GOD SAVE
THE EGGS!

and other stories we might have told you

Woody and Susan Roland

Outskirts Press, Inc.
Denver, Colorado

Para Kari, Krista, Norma y Toty. ¡Gracias por ser
parte de la aventura!
and
Gary, Jack, Joe and Mark. You know who you
are and what you mean to us.

TABLE OF CONTENTS

The Story Before the Other Stories

Most of these stories were written to friends who have prayed for our ministry over the years. Without them we would not have lived many of these experiences. We certainly wouldn't have written about them! Thank you for standing with us all these years.

All of the stories were written by both of us. However, we do not want to confuse you unnecessarily with the change of "voice." The stories written from Susan's perspective are identified as such in the table of contents. She wouldn't want you to think that she has jumped off skyscrapers or bitten her sister. She certainly would not want to communicate that she reads in the bathroom!

A few special thanks are in order. Thank

you Suzie, Lori, Carolyn, Kari and Rick for looking at these essays, sharing your honest opinions and asking the hard questions. Thanks for correcting our most apparent grammatical errors. The remaining mistakes are ours and we take full responsibility.

"You will do foolish things, but do them with en-thusiasm."

Colette

Grandma Rode A Pig

I wish I had been there the day my grand-mother rode the pig. I should have been present for such a momentous occasion.

I would not make something like this up. It really happened, and I am pretty sure that Grandma Blanche Roland would not rest well if she knew that I was sharing this story with you.

My grandmother was what was referred to in those days as a "holiness woman." She be-lieved that what you did, said and wore were important reflections of your actual state of grace with God. Riding pigs was not consid-ered to be a normal part of the holiness ex-perience. Especially in a dress, in front of a man, even if he had been your husband for forty years.

It certainly wasn't something that you

talked about with others.

It seems that my grandfather had asked Blanche to help him separate an especially difficult sow from the rest of the pigs. All he asked her to do was stand in the door between the swine and dairy sides of the barn while he got the rest of the herd to run outside. The sow in question became rather excited and began looking for alternative routes of escape as most of her companions escaped to the pig pasture.

Now, one of the characteristics of older holiness women is their absolute abhorrence of jeans, slacks or pants. They share the general understanding that if God had meant a woman to wear trousers, He wouldn't have invented dresses. With that in mind, my grandmother had gone to the barn in her normal clothing.

I personally believe the sow may have had a genuine conversion experience when she saw the light below Blanche's hemline. That pig headed for it like a sinner seeking salvation.

What the sow could see clearly on the other side of my grandmother was something that must have warmed her heart every bit as much as John Wesley's was at Aldersgate – an open barn door. There could have been no finer sight, and there was no stopping her now.

As the pig went between Blanche's legs, it lifted up. At the same time, Grandma's dress stretched and tightened down. Without a great deal of forethought, my grandmother found herself riding a pig backwards about to experience what was on the "other side."

Considering that he had been trying to corner this particular sow, it was probably good that my grandfather chased through the barn and out the door after my grandmother and her newly acquired steed.

Once the pig was free of the barn, it ran up the road to the other farm buildings. When it got to the lawn area between the orchard and the house, it began to run in circles with my grandmother still mounted, crying out, "Joe, Joe!"

It is at this point that Grandpa Roland committed a serious matrimonial error.

Rather than trying to reach over and somehow get Blanche off the pig's back, he stopped and laughed. Not the delicate "I am afraid I have caught you at an embarrassing moment" laugh, but the "this is too funny to be true" kind of laugh that only tends to infuriate real holiness people. After all, humor is a bit too close to sin to be tolerated comfortably.

My grandmother realized that she should have never allowed herself to be used in such a way. Finally, as the pig completed one more circuit, she leaned over and fell onto the grass.

I have been told (and can easily believe) that she didn't talk to Grandpa for two weeks.

One of the reasons I wish that I had been there the day Grandma Roland rode the pig is that it became one of those stories that would always be repeated when Grandma was just out of hearing range. I can still see my uncle telling the story and laughing so hard he cried.

If Grandma had caught him telling it, he would have cried in a different way.

Stories were always part of our family. Almost every Sunday of my childhood, we either "went visiting" or had someone come and sit with us for awhile. The stories would begin once the food was consumed, the price of milk discussed and the latest news communicated. There were no rules about who could tell the stories (we all knew them by heart), but there were always some who were known for telling the right stories in the right way. My Uncle Phil could tell a story. Uncle Jim could tell the funniest stories with a straight face (he also had a pair of great-Grandfathers named Ole Olson and Sven Svenson, but that is a whole other story). My father could tell stories that were so funny or so sad that you could get choked up either way.

My grandfather could tell stories. Of course, he never got to tell the one about Grandma on the pig. At least he never told it within earshot of her.

It has been occasionally said of me that I tell stories. While some people intend to subtly insult me when they say that I am a "story teller," I take it as a compliment. I follow in the tradition of my uncles, father and grandfather. More than that, I believe I follow in the tradition of God.

GOD SAVE THE EGGS!

Eugene Peterson wrote, "The biblical story comprises other literary forms – sermons and genealogies, prayers and letters, poems and proverbs – but story carries them all in its capacious and organically intricate plot. Moses told stories; Jesus told stories; the four Gospel writers presented their good news in the form of stories. And the Holy Spirit weaves all this storytelling into the vast and holy literary architecture that reveals God to us as Father, Son and Holy Spirit in the way He chooses to make Himself known. Story. To get the revelation right, we enter the story." (*Leap Over A Wall*, Eugene Peterson, p. 3.)

I like what John Eldredge wrote in *The Sacred Romance* (p. 39): "Life is not a list of propositions, it is a series of dramatic scenes...Story is the language of the heart. Our souls speak not in the naked facts of mathematics or the abstract propositions of systematic theology; they speak the images and emotions of story."

I wish I could have been there the day Grandma Roland rode the pig, but I am especially glad I was there when the story was shared. Each time it's told, she becomes alive again with all of her personality traits, religion, rules and life force. If reincarnation exists, it is only through the stories we tell.

An old Scottish missionary in Bolivia once explained the Lord's Supper in a way that finally made sense to me. He said that what Christians call Holy Communion is really a continuation of an old Middle Eastern tradition. After a man died, his friends would gather together on a regular basis to enjoy a special supper where the main topic of conversation would be their deceased companion. Many times, in the midst of the stories and humorous accounts, the deceased man would almost seem to come alive again in their midst.

That is what the Lord's Supper should be! Stories that make Him come alive.

I am not ashamed of occasionally telling a few stories. I admit that I love seeing people's eyes open up in surprise or crinkle in laughter at just the right moment. It is who I am, and it is who the people I tell stories about once were.

In some ways, our whole missionary adventure these past thirty years has been a story. It certainly has been an adventure. It has also been fun, challenging and occasionally a little frightening.

Of course, all of this reminds me of a story...

"Cherish your visions and your dreams as they are the children of your soul..."

Napoleon Hill

Career Goals

It was never my career goal to be a missionary. For a long time, I didn't even want to be a Christian.

I blame the past 30 years on three people: Harry Woods, Bob Sawtell and Tom Burt. To my knowledge, only two of them even knew each other in passing. I seriously doubt if they met together and discussed how they would ruin my life, but sometimes it feels like they did.

As a young boy, I had the "privilege" of living around the corner from a retired missionary named Harry Woods. Harry and his wife were treacherous Christians. They did not preach. They did not cajole. Instead, they baked cookies and told wonderful stories about their years in the Orient.

Because of them, even before I became a Christian, I knew there were some missionaries

WOODY AND SUSAN ROLAND

who had lived their lives to the fullest.

* * *

Bob Sawtell told wonderful stories, but he also asked questions.

In November of 1973, I begged rides and hitchhiked from Texas to Minnesota with the purpose of asking for Bob's blessing to marry his daughter Susan. When I arrived at the Sawtell home, Bob met with me in his office. The roll-top desk, books on the shelves and leather sofa were all impressive to a long-haired college student.

When I announced the purpose of my visit, Bob began to ask questions.

"Woody, what do you plan to do in life?"

"Well, I am going to drop out of college, marry Su and work while she finishes her last semester."

I seem to remember that Bob swallowed hard at this point, but continued with his questions. "What are you planning on doing after she finishes?"

"We plan to move back to Texas and I will finish my last two semesters of study and Susan will work as a nurse."

I believe Bob thought I was getting a good deal by having Su work two semesters for my one, but he did not allow himself to get distracted by details.

"After you both finish college what do you plan to do?"

GOD SAVE THE EGGS!

Fortunately, Su and I had talked about this subject in one of our many long-distance phone calls between Texas and the land of 10,000 loons.

"We would both like to spend some time studying the Word of God in a Bible School or Seminary."

"Well, Woody, what do you want to do with your life after that?"

I had no idea. I really think my career goal at this point in life was to wake up next to Susan in the same bed! I was tired of living on opposite sides of the United States.

At that critical moment, I looked over Bob's shoulder at the filing cabinet behind him. On it were hanging several MISSIONARY PRAYER CARDS. I was desperate and an idea began to form in my mind.

I should explain at this point, in the two years I had dated Susan, I had engaged in the normal sparring conversations with my future father-in-law. I say "normal" because, as the father of three daughters, I now understand some of the feelings that surface when a young man begins to date your daughter. You really want the best for her and he, no matter who he is, is never the best.

Now, as a result of those hours of conversation, I knew Bob had great respect for missions and missionaries. With fear and trembling, I made my next strategic gambit.

"Dr. Sawtell, I think Susan and I would like to try cross-cultural ministry."

WOODY AND SUSAN ROLAND

Bob looked up and asked me if I was serious. Even though I could hear the saw as it cut through the floor below me, I responded affirmatively.

"That's great, Woody! You have my blessing."

Afterwards, I told Susan I had good news and bad news. The good news was that we could get married. The bad news was we were going to be missionaries.

Please note that Bob never asked me what we were going to do after we were missionaries.

Some days I wish he had.

* * *

Tom Burt didn't tell that many stories and asked less pointed questions than Bob, but he did listen.

Tom and I were roommates in Texas. We shared interests in aviation, music and a love for Jesus Christ. We also talked together at night as we were going to sleep.

It is natural for young men in college to share about their dreams. For those of us who survived the 60's and became Christians in the early 70's, it also seemed natural to talk about how we were going to change the world.

Tom listened to my dreams.

One night, Tom challenged me by responding to something I had said. After an evening's discussion of the world's evils and what should be done to change them, Tom asked me, "If you are serious, why don't you really do it?"

For once in my life, I couldn't think of a decent excuse.

Now, here we are thirty years later.

It could have been worse. I could have lived around the corner from a friendly mortician instead of Rev. Woods. My future father-in-law could have had his daughter's financial security be his primary interest. And my roommate could have kept quiet.

It could have been worse, but it wouldn't have been as interesting.

"I am thankful for laughter, except when milk comes out of my nose."

Woody Allen

Can't Help Laughing

I can't help it. Sometimes even the most serious moments in Christianity make me laugh.

When we had lived in Bolivia for about seven months, it was my privilege to perform the first baptisms for our young church. Many people have worked faithfully for years and not seen disciples formed and growing. God must have known I needed the extra encouragement to keep going.

Because this was to be my first baptism in La Paz, my missionary mentor, Wes Steffen, suggested that we should do it together. He had some Christians from his church who wanted to be baptized and thought it would be good idea for us to have a combined Sunday afternoon service.

It was a special joy to see people in whom

we had invested so much make this public testimony of their faith.

Still, when a businessman from Wes' church stepped through the side door and moved toward the baptismal, I knew we were not only standing in water – we were in deep weeds. To this day I have rarely seen someone with such a large tummy. He looked like he had arrived at "nine months pregnant" and just kept growing.

Wes asked the usual questions for a baptism and the man responded properly. I put my hand behind his back and began to lay his considerable bulk back into the water.

This is where the difference between Wes' doctrine and mine became evident.

Once the man was lying in the water, it was obvious a significant island of belly had not made it underwater.

I believe the symbol of baptism is actually more important that how much water you get on you in the process. Wes was concerned that some of the young Bolivian believers might not understand my doctrinal subtlety. So, when I began to lift the man out of the water, Wes stage-whispered, "Woody, he is not fully immersed!"

I remember looking at our victim and responding, "Well, what do you suggest we do?"

"We need to make waves."

"What?"

"Waves. Push with your free hand and make waves."

I should explain the gentleman now had his

eyes open and small bubbles were escaping from his mouth. He probably believed that he was coming close to fully identifying with the death and burial of our Lord.

Still, I was the new kid on the block so I made waves.

Finally, a small tsunami splashed across his dry acreage. Without consulting Wes, I pulled the near drowning victim up.

I was rewarded by "one of those stares" from the businessman meant to let me know this had all been my fault.

Wes failed to explain to his church members the intricacies of the doctrinal issue we had faced.

* * *

Years later, our now growing church had traveled to a mountain river to baptize a large group of new believers.

Miriam, a young psychologist, decided at the last moment that she would also like to identify with her Lord through being immersed. The other leaders agreed Miriam could do this, and she made her preparations. She appeared at the river's edge in what appeared to be her house robe.

I was not actually baptizing this day. Instead, I preached a small message on the subject of baptism and was now watching with the others as two elders in the church lowered the good saints into the frigid, mountain stream.

WOODY AND SUSAN ROLAND

All went well until the psychologist stepped between the two men. They asked the questions. Miriam responded. They lowered her into the water. They lifted her up.

Her previously modest gown had now become transparent. As the two church leaders looked towards the crowd at river's edge with properly spiritual expressions, we looked back at a lady who had decided not to get any of her undergarments wet and was now effectually naked.

Since the tumbling river was so loud, it was impossible to actually speak with the three in the middle of the stream. Because the leaders were still not looking at the young lady, this meant I was reduced to sign language to communicate the moral situation we were now literally facing.

The crucial moment came when one of the men finally realized he needed to look down at Miriam.

I have heard of groups that baptize people more than once. Until this moment, I hadn't seen it. Miriam was pushed into the water again. When she tried to get up (still not realizing, so to speak, her own level of transparency), the largest elder simply held her in the river.

Finally, we were able to get a towel to midstream and continue with the service.

* * *

While taking an educational leave from Bolivia, we lived for over a year in Duluth, Minnesota. During that time we had the privilege of seeing a father, mother and two teenagers become Christians. When it came time for the family to be baptized, they asked the pastor of the church we attended together if I could perform the ceremony.

This caused some consternation from the church board because I was not ordained in their particular denomination. Still, Pastor Fred thought it would be a good idea and asked me to perform two of the four baptisms.

Since Duluth is located on the shores of Lake Superior, I was concerned the water in the church baptismal might be pretty chilly. Fred assured me the baptismal was connected to the church's hot water system and that I had nothing to worry about.

On Sunday morning, as I stepped into the water, it was immediately apparent to my toes that Fred had not been able to fulfill his promise. Something had gone wrong and the water was freezing.

Because I knew several members of the church were still concerned about my baptizing anyone on a Sunday morning, I managed to conceal my discomfort. David, the seventeen-year-old that I was baptizing, was not as hypocritical.

He grimaced when his feet went in the water. However, there came a point when he could no longer refrain from saying, "_ _ _ _, that's cold!" Unfortunately, his voice carried to the very back of the sanctuary.

Now, more nervous than I needed to be, I asked David if he had trusted in Jesus Christ as his personal Savior. He responded with additional complaints about the water in addition to his very sincere testimony. As I lowered him to the water I proceeded to say, "Entonces, te bautizo en el nombre del Padre, del Hijo..."

I had slipped into Spanish!

Not only was someone beside the pastor baptizing on a Sunday morning; not only was the young man being baptized swearing in the baptismal; in addition to all that, I was speaking in tongues!

I looked out at the congregation and stopped mid-sentence. A very serious-looking group of Minnesota Baptists looked up at me. No explanation was going to suffice. It was better to get the whole frigid experience over with.

* * *

Occasionally, late at night, I still wonder what happened to "the large tummy," Miriam and David. I have lost contact with all of them. I can't help wondering if the manner in which they were baptized impacted their Christian walk negatively. Still, after praying for them, I can't help laughing. You would, too, if you had been there.

"Judge of your natural character by what you do in your dreams."

Ralph Waldo Emerson

A Dream Come True

We co-own a cabin in a remote, mountainous area of Costa Rica which has become a wonderful get-away spot for us. It also serves as a youth and leadership retreat site and, at times, even a honeymoon cabin.

We pay Rodrigo, a local gardener, about $25 a month to keep up the yard for us. During our first year of ownership, we went out of our way to make friends with Rodrigo. As our friendship deepened, Rodrigo opened up with us and told us of his wife's struggles with clinical depression. Because she rarely accompanied her husband on his visits to the cabin, I had only met her once.

Woody and I began to pray for Nena, Rodrigo and their family. We decided that if Nena showed up with Rodrigo while we were at the cabin, we would invite them in for coffee. Not long afterwards we went to stay overnight at the cabin. Early that Saturday morning, Rodrigo showed up to mow the lawn. Surprisingly, Nena came with him. She is a very shy person, but she actually came up to the door and asked to borrow a rake to help Rodrigo.

After I fetched the rake, I began to chat with Nena. I mentioned that we would love to invite them in for coffee. As we stood on the porch, Nena began to share her life story with me. She was amazingly open about her experiences as an inpatient at a psychiatric hospital, struggling with severe postpartum depression. Several times in her conversation she mentioned her desire to know God. As I prepared to go in to fix coffee, I mentioned to her that I had a pamphlet that tells what the Bible says about knowing God personally. I suggested she look at it while I put the coffee on.

When Nena took the tract from me, she opened to a page with a diagram showing man's separation from God. Before I could even turn to get out the coffee, she began to cry.

"What's wrong, Nena?" I asked.

"This picture! I know just what it is! Several years ago I had a vivid dream of this picture. See the person on this side of the chasm? That is me. And on the other side is God. There is a big chasm separating us and I am ready to fall into it and be lost forever. But, I have one very important question. In my dream, there was a bridge that spans the gap between God and me. Susana, what is that bridge and how can I find it?"

I decided the coffee could wait a minute.

Nena wanted to know every single detail and hear every single Bible verse. Before we could get to the last page, Nena excitedly interrupted me.

"I know I am a sinner. I know that Jesus died and rose again so that He could be the bridge to bring me back to God. Can I pray right now to tell Him that I want to trust Him as my Savior? I want to do that so badly!"

I felt like saying, "Just wait! We haven't gotten to that page yet!"

But, instead, I said, "Sure, Nena. I know that God would be so pleased to respond to your prayer."

As she prayed her own simple sinner's prayer, I shook my head in wonder of God's work in her life.

After she prayed, I added my own prayer of rejoicing over this miraculous new birth. I turned to Nena and said, "You know what your name means, right? It means a little girl or baby girl. Now you are a new baby in Jesus and He is so eager to have you read His Word and learn from Him."

As I stepped into the little kitchen to finally put the coffee pot on, I heard Nena run with excitement to her husband. I think Rodrigo was a bit taken aback with her enthusiasm.

WOODY AND SUSAN ROLAND

She said, "Remember, Rodrigo, my dream about being separated from God?!? Susana told me exactly what the Bible says about that and now I know the bridge is Jesus!"

Nena continues to grow in her faith. Rodrigo isn't far behind. He can't deny God's touch on his wife's life!

"Life is not lost by dying; life is lost minute by minute, day by dragging day, in all the thousand small uncaring ways."

Stephen Vincent Benét

Finding the Lost

It is always great to find something that we thought was lost. The experience helps us to appreciate what we have in a special way.

In 2004, we had a family from Rochester, Minnesota, visit the Multiplication Center. Chuck and Pat Treder brought their teenagers, Jill and Luke, with them to see a bit of Costa Rica and help fix up some of the rooms in San Isidro. They also lost, or almost lost, a few things while they were here.

On Tuesday night, after a long day of work, we decided to see one of the traditional Roman Catholic processions that occur during Holy Week in Costa Rica. We had been told the procession would begin at 6:30 p.m. in the center of San Isidro, so we loaded up the car (sticking Luke in the luggage area) and drove down to the main square. Sure enough, we saw "Roman soldiers" getting into a bus – a definite sign that we were about to see a procession. Since we thought we had a bit of time, we went into the cathedral for a few minutes.

While there was a little activity toward the front of the building, nothing indicated that a procession was getting ready to burst forth through the front doors anytime soon. We decided to leave and ask a few questions.

In front of the building we asked about the procession. "Certainly there is a procession! It starts from a church two kilometers south of San Isidro." Okay! This was more like it. We all piled back in the car and headed south of town. Once again we asked about the procession. "Yes, that procession starts at a church about two hundred meters west of here. We corrected our path and found... nothing. No faux Roman soldiers. No candles or torches. No images being carried on men's shoulders.

We seemed to have lost the procession.

After wandering around on dark country roads trying to act like we knew what we were doing for the Treder's sake ("Well, it is fairly easy to lose the occasional procession, you know."), we decided to return to San Isidro to check things out. After all, in Latin America you never know when a random religious procession could just turn up.

Sure enough, once we arrived in town we

saw some emergency lights blinking down a side road. It had to be the police driving a car in front of the pilgrims! Nope. False alarm.

A radio station was setting up their portable broadcasting van in the main square. Although we were already headed back home, Susan challenged my manhood and insisted I ask one of the men if there wasn't going to be a march this evening. "Yes," he replied, "the procession begins at 8:30 this evening and leaves from this church."

We were too tired to wait that long. Time to get back to the Center and get to bed. There was a lot on the Treder's schedule for the next day.

Driving up the road to the Multiplication Center, not two hundred meters from the main entrance to the property, we were suddenly confronted by a parade of Roman soldiers with spears and torches carrying an image of the Christ with a whip and followed by a mass of the citizenry of San Isidro. They must have wondered why the car jammed with gringos was laughing uproariously at them as they walked somberly past us.

The next morning we were on the road by 6:10 a.m. in order to get the Treders to their tour of several spots in central Costa Rica. A full four weeks before, Susan had arranged the tour, reconfirmed it several times and paid for the whole package. Chuck, Pat, Jill and Luke were going to see a volcano, waterfalls, a butterfly "farm" and the natural jungle around the

WOODY AND SUSAN ROLAND

Sarapiqui River. This was going to be great!

We arrived at the hotel where we had arranged to have the tour company pick them up at 6:40 am.

"Are you the people here for the tour?" the rather dour hotel clerk asked me in Spanish.

"Yes, these are the people!"

"Well, the bus arrived a few minutes ago and has already left. We are not responsible – you were late."

Occasionally, my *"How to Deal with Recalcitrant Airline Personnel"* voice finds use in other areas of our ministry.

"I am sorry, but you will please note that we are here talking at 6:32am and the pick up is not scheduled until 6:40am. I think that you need to come up with some solution that could possibly still save your job – please."

I always try to be polite with recalcitrant people.

"Why, yes sir! I just happen to have the emergency phone number for the tour company and would be glad to call them for you." Who said behavior modification did not work?

Rrrring. "Hello? What? You missed the bus? It's not my fault. I guess you lost your only chance to go on the tour today."

Hmm, we seemed to be losing a lot here recently.

Once again, I employed my *Airline Personnel Voice*.

"Yes! Of course! Now that I am fully awake and the alcohol from last night is wearing off, I certainly see your point. I will call the bus for you right away."

My new friend, the hotel reception-type guy, indicated that I had a phone call on another line. I hung up on my newly friendly and helpful emergency-tour-type guy and answered the other line.

"Woody, this is Susan. You have to take the Treders to the Irazu Hotel so that they can catch their bus. You have to go *now*!"

Finding this lost tour was starting to feel a lot like finding that lost procession.

Upon arrival at the Irazu Hotel, we were first told that they couldn't go on the tour; it was all full. By this time, every conversation seemed to require the *Airline Personnel Voice*. The tour operator finally responded, "Well, yes, they can go on the tour. You need to know that none of this is our fault. After all, the person who sold this tour does not really work with us."

Menacing laser eyes were added to the now full-blown *Airline Personnel Voice*.

Backing down, they said, "Of course, we don't want to argue about this. Hurry and get them on the bus."

The Treders ended up having a great day. The tour company called and apologized profusely for their error. Holy Week and its processions continued. The work the Treders came to do at the Multiplication Center was finished beautifully.

After taking Chuck, Pat and their kids to the airport, we decided to drive our jeep up to the end of our road and take a little walk. Since we always like to see what is just around the next bend in the path, the "little walk" ended up being a bit more extensive than we had anticipated. After entering into primary forest, we kept hearing water. The path took us through some incredible scenery and the sound of the water kept encouraging us forward. Finally, when we thought we couldn't go any further, a beautiful waterfall came into view, framed by trees that must have been three hundred years old.

We had found something that we hadn't realized was lost. The joy of finding it, of making this unexpected discovery, made the effort of getting there worthwhile – in spite of the man-eating chiggers.

There was something else lost this week. When Su and I and the Treders were in the Catholic Church in San Isidro waiting for the "lost procession," I noticed that one of the usual images was not on display. During most of the year, the Cathedral has a rather hideous image of the Christ on display inside of a crystal coffin. It tends to attract a lot of attention. I know, because every time I go in, I look at it. It's kind of like pushing my tongue against a sore tooth. I don't know why I do it, but I do.

During this Holy Week, the church decided that it would take the figure out of the coffin. In fact, that coffin is there right now – empty.

I guess it is a lot like another tomb found empty almost two thousand years ago. I can only imagine that some of the soldiers not on duty *that* Sunday morning must have wondered how you could lose the cadaver of a Jewish holy man. They probably used the early equivalent of the *Recalcitrant Airline Personnel Voice* on their trembling buddies who had been on duty. They certainly helped come up with some type of story to cover their embarrassing loss.

My guess is that the figure of Jesus will be back in its coffin in San Isidro on Monday. However, the truth is, those Roman soldiers never did find that lost body. I am glad they didn't. It is the only hope for lost people like me.

"A good puzzle should demand the exercise of our best wit and ingenuity... it sometimes happens that a kind of natural cunning and sagacity is of considerable value."

Henry Ernest Dudeney

Adventures at Ralph's

had just returned from Manila where I had met with the other members of International Teams' Executive Team. The meetings were long, but profitable. Sometimes people think of all this travel as some type of adventure, but I really think you can find as much adventure in going to the local grocery store.

I know I did.

On a Friday night, I arrived at Los Angeles International Airport after twenty-five hours of travel. At the airport I called some friends of ours, Al and Nancy Mendez, who live in the L.A. area. They weren't home, so I left a message, telling them I would be staying at a nearby hotel, grabbing about six hours of sleep, before continuing my journey to Costa Rica.

As I walked into the hotel to check in, one

of the two young ladies in reception said, "Oh, Mr. Roland, a lady just called for you." I responded, "Great! That must have been Nancy." The young lady who had taken the phone call said, "No, I believe it was a Susan." To which I responded, without thinking, "Oh, that one is my wife."

Sometimes it doesn't help to try to explain your way out of the situation when you receive *that* type of look.

My stomach told me I was hungry. I had noticed a restaurant around the corner called "Woody's." For some reason, that seemed to be the right place to go, but I had no U.S. cash. So I decided to go to Ralph's Grocery, a store a couple of blocks away that I believed would have an ATM.

I ignored the expressions on the faces of the hotel staff as I walked through the lobby. Once you've lost your testimony, it's hard to get it back again.

Between the produce and bakery departments, Ralph's had two ATMs and one of those fancy phone lines that allow you to connect directly with a bank's 24-hour customer service. I was taking my bank card out of my wallet when it slipped out of my sleep-deprived fingers.

I can still see it as if it were in slow motion: it bounced twice on the counter, twisted in the air and went directly into the slot for trash. The slot that is purposely so small that no one can see your check book balance or account information... the slot that human fingers cannot get into!

I turned to the couple using the second machine and said dully, "My bank card just went into the trash slot." The lady responded (and I am NOT making this up!), "Like wow! That is so totally incredible!" Her husband had the common sense to only say, "Whoa, dude!"

I told you I was in California, right?

I knew the only man who could help me at this point was the manager of Ralph's Grocery. I asked one of the cashiers to page him for me. As I got back to the machine, I heard an announcement over the P.A. system," Would Mr. Smith please go to the ATM by produce? There is an emergency."

Apparently, she had detected my level of desperation.

The manager arrived within a few minutes. The surfing couple was still with me, and she immediately began to explain what had happened. The manager responded (and once again, I am not making this up), "Bad luck, guy."

I was starting to feel a need to go into my cross-cultural communication mode.

Mr. Smith did eventually inform me that I would have to call the bank on their customer phone line because he did not have the key that would open the trash bin. I do not want to go into all the details, but I will say that I spent over an hour on the phone. I spoke to one customer service rep and two supervisors. The last one was on the east coast. The best advice they could give me was that I could either leave the card in the trash and hope the people who found it would destroy it, or, I could try to bang the machine with my hand which would set off an internal alarm. This would either summon the people who usually serviced the machine or bring the police. If it brought the police, I would probably be arrested.

Even in my jet-lagged state, I knew there had to be another, more optimistic, option.

It occurred to me at some point during my conversations with the supervisor on the east coast that I might be able to get something very thin down into the slot. So, after politely declining her suggestion to set off the alarm, I went back to the manager of Ralph's and told him that I was going to try to get the card out myself and didn't want any of his employees calling the police when they saw me working on the machine. He responded, "Wouldn't think of it, man."

Somewhere in cosmetics I found two long, thin nail files. For some reason, the flashlights were in the liquor department. I decided not to ask the manager why. When I went up to the counter to buy my new tools, the young lady who checked me out asked, "Are you the dude that is trying to break into the cash machine?"

Obviously, my reputation was growing.

With flashlight in mouth and two files in

hand, I peered into the slot and saw my pre-cious card! It was right on a pile of paper that had kept it from falling into the deeper abyss of the trash bin. It was almost within reach.

"Almost" is the key word here. I found that my newly-purchased nail files were about 1 1/2 inches too short.

Back to cosmetics for a package of emery boards and a side trip to house supplies for some duct tape. Somehow, I just knew my luck would change if I had duct tape. Once again back to the check out line. This time I distinctly remember one in the growing crowd using the term "old guy" in reference to me.

Is no one in California over 40?

I managed to duct tape two emery boards to each of my nail files. Once again the flash-light went into my mouth and my tools went into the dark slot. This time I actually got the card between my manufactured pincers and began to draw it up. I was almost home – then, when the card was almost to the narrow slot, it slipped and fell back into the trash, this time deeper than ever.

I don't think that I've mentioned that a crowd had formed around me. I think I was actually developing a bond with the motor-cycle guy with his rather obese girlfriend in the motorized cart. They were at least as old as I am.

I may not be an intelligent missionary, but I am persistent. I wasn't going to fail in front of such a cloud of witnesses. I redid the file/emery boards/duct-taped pincers so the ends had duct tape with the sticky side out. Manipulating this contraption with the very tips of my fingers I was able to once again get a hold of my precious card. This time it came up to the dreaded slot where I was able to twist it and grab it with two fingers.

People clapped. I am not kidding.

All told, my adventure at Ralph's only took two hours. In the meantime, Woody's had closed, along with all the other nearby restaurants. However, my rather extensive exploration of Ralph's had revealed to me the location of those wax covered donuts I like. You know, the ones where they make the wax look like chocolate. I can assure you that I didn't try to explain to the hotel receptionists where I had been.

I had the feeling they wouldn't believe me.

"Religion needs a baptism of horse sense."
Billy Sunday

Our Lady of the Blessed Bazooka

C osta Ricans, like all inhabitants of the planet Earth, have some interesting religious customs. Each August, many Ticos make a pilgrimage to the Virgin of Los Angeles in Cartago. As I found out a few years ago, a pilgrimage is not something that you want to be forced to do as an Evangelical. It requires far too much effort and does not provide nearly enough religious rewards.

A few times each year, we celebrate something in the town of Tres Rios that deals with the Catholic Church religious calendar. However, I still remain ignorant as to the true nature and meaning of these holy days. After speaking with some of our neighborhood friends, I am comforted by the fact that I do not seem to be the only one who suffers from a lack of information.

WOODY AND SUSAN ROLAND

There is one thing that all of us (including Bagel, our trusty beagle) are very aware of: there is one holy day that can best be celebrated by discharging large of amounts of gunpowder in small cannons. Humor me and try to imagine a strange cosmic brew of Arnold Schwarzenegger and the Pope.

Bagel, who is usually adamant about going on her evening walk, has even been refusing to go outside during the evening cannonade. She hides in some corner of the house, forcing me to look for her and drag her outside.

With nothing else to go on, I have decided that we must be celebrating the festival that I affectionately call, "Our Lady of the Blessed Bazooka."

During the festival of the Blessed Bazooka, we begin and end our days with the thunderous sound of cannons. I think this may have something to do with the fact that, since Costa Rica has no army, Ticos do not get to live out certain, natural male fantasies. As I was once told by a military officer, "I have the best job in the world. I get to blow things up!"

Unfortunately for mankind in general, I think he was serious.

This is not the only holiday that Ticos celebrate by discharging large-bore firearms. In fact, in one town that we often go through, they seem to have a semi-perpetual celebration that can require random cannon firing. On more than one occasion, we have been passing through the town center with our whole family when a nearby cannon was fired.

I did mention that Bagel does not care for the sound of explosions, didn't I?

Unfortunately, when a beagle opposed to the sound of gunfire is placed in close proximity to the sound of an exploding cannon, he will often fire off his or her own "biological cannon." It is even more unfortunate if this biological cannon is fired when the dog is seated in the front seat on one of her owner's laps.

This is still a source of some resentment on Susan's part.

I was once in Tenancingo, Mexico, when they celebrated their equivalent of Our Lady of the Blessed Bazooka.

It is a long story, and I know you are surprised that I don't tell it here. However, knowing that I blew up the kitchen of one our missionaries should let you know that I entered into the celebrations with full gusto and great cultural awareness.

I am still not sure if I understand the full religious meaning of the Blessed Bazooka. However, I know that I will celebrate it next year with more paper towels and wet wash cloths in our jeep.

So, from our family to yours, we hope the only explosions you hear during this celebration of Our Lady of the Blessed Bazooka are from gunpowder, and that all cannons fired at you will be of the distinctly non-organic variety.

> "The grinding of the intellect is for most people as painful as the dentist's drill."
>
> *Leonard Woolf*

Dental Stories Included

Caution: The following story contains graphic descriptions of dental experiences. Individuals with high blood pressure and cardiac conditions are warned.

Susan and I recently celebrated 26 years since we first went to live in La Paz, Bolivia. So many experiences; so many lives transformed by the power of God; so many adventures... too many trips to Latin American dentists.

Last week I was forced to make another one of "those" visits.

I want to make something clear. There are good dentists out there. Perhaps a few of you reading this report are dentists. Susan and I have had the privilege of being served by several excellent dentists. Unfortunately, they were all in the States.

Actually, I think my luck with dentists (or

lack thereof) began in the United States. As a child, I was taken by my parents to an ancient DDS in the small town where my uncle lived. I can't remember many details of those experiences, but my older sister trembles and turns paler than normal when she recalls those office visits.

I trust her.

Later on, my parents found a dentist whose sole qualification (from my childhood perspective) was that he had played a bit of baseball with my grandfather. I imagine most dental professionals need to fulfill more requirements in the modern era.

This "gentleman" seemed inured to the pain I experienced in his chair. So, on one particular visit, I made the proactive and unilateral decision to help him develop empathy for his younger patients. When he put his nicotine stained fingers in my mouth, I bit his thumb. Since I knew that I would be punished if he managed to extricate his hand from my oral clamp, I held on with the considerable strength my talkative nature had already developed in my jaws.

If I remember correctly, it took both his assistant and receptionist to get me to release my intended prey. I know I learned several new vocabulary words that day which my parents had failed to teach me until that moment in life.

All of these memories came to mind last week when I went to visit a dentist in San Jose.

GOD SAVE THE EGGS!

Dr. Jose Wong practices with his father. The Wong family has had an office in the same spot in San Jose for 50 years, and it certainly looks like it. The area is better known for prostitution than up-and-coming professional practices. Still, as Jose says, "The overhead is low."

I bet.

I wish I could tell you that my experience was, well, palatable. Unfortunately, I feel compelled to share the truth.

After waiting for almost three hours in the Wong's hallway (there is no waiting room), I was finally led to a chair that looked like it had been first used in the early Eisenhower administration. I did not hold it against the doctor that some of the equipment was literally stuck together with duct tape. Several of my engineering friends from college would have been proud of the effective usage of this important product. Still, there seemed to be a general "seediness" about the place that did not inspire my confidence.

Jose Wong is nothing if not polite. In fact, he often repeats the phrase, "Mucho gusto"... "pleasure to see you." This would be okay, but he seems to repeat the statement at random moments in the conversation. Example: "Dr. Wong! There is blood flowing freely from the oral wounds inflicted on me in your office." "Ah, Woody. Mucho gusto, mucho gusto."

There is friendly. And there is macabre. I will leave the decision to your criteria.

After a cursory examination, Jose explained

to me that I needed to have one of my old fillings replaced. While I felt a tinge of regret about this since it was a souvenir of my old friend the baseball player, the pain in my mouth told me it was absolutely necessary. So, I agreed to the procedure.

The first thing that Jose asked me was whether I wanted to have any Novocain. When I asked him if there would be any pain, he replied honestly, "Yes." I replied just as honestly, "Yes, I believe I would like to have Novocain."

After the first shot, I told the dentist that I still had a great deal of feeling in the area in which he intended to work. He replied that he would just try a bit of drilling to see if there really was any sensitivity. The extended arch of my back and "electric shock jerk" of my entire body seemed to convince him of the need for an additional shot.

Three injections later the entire right side of my head was numb, but I was still experiencing excruciating pain in the general area of Dr. Wong's excavations. Jose, ever the professional, compensated for the lack of response to his injections by leaning against my chest and repeating "mucho gusto" or other phrases to the same effect.

When we finally finished, Dr. Wong thanked me for coming in, let me know once again that it was a pleasure to have seen me, and asked me if I normally had a silly grin with drool spilling out of it.

GOD SAVE THE EGGS!

Still, all of my recent experiences could not compare to a dental adventure I had years ago in Bolivia.

One of my team members, Rob Brynjolfson, decided he needed to have his wisdom teeth removed. When he asked me for a suggestion of a dentist, I told him about Esperanza Aid, a woman who had been highly recommended to me. He made the appointment and asked me to accompany him.

Esperanza, whose name means "hope," would have been better served by a sign in front of her office which stated, "Abandon all hope, ye who enter here." When my team-mate's number came up, we walked across the warped wooden floor and into the inner sanctum of dental horror.

The chair dated from the near-Incan period of South American history. The drill looked to be foot-operated. The dentist was less than five feet tall and might have weighed 98 pounds. I wasn't sure if we had found ourselves in a piece of literature by Dante, or, if we were in the Kingdom of Oz.

She already had the scalpel in her hand when she asked us if we wanted to have No-vocain. When Rob replied affirmatively, she told us that a shot would be an extra charge. At the very least Latin dentists are honest about charges and pain. We agreed to the additional cost and waited as she drew up the medication in a glass syringe that she had probably bought from my first family dentist.

45

After drawing the medicine, she proceeded to place a drop of it in the mouth of my co-worker.

That is right. A drop.

I am not sure what happened to the rest of that anesthetic, but it was still in the syringe when we left the office.

After asking my companion to open his mouth, she began the procedure. It was obvious from the first cut that one drop of Novocain was not going to be sufficient. Still, she kept at it. She was honest and persistent.

Dr. Aid finally managed to get pliers on the offending tooth. Unfortunately, when she started to pull, it wasn't Rob's tooth that came out. Instead, his entire torso came out of the chair.

It was at that moment that I understood why I had been invited to come in with Rob. The dentist indicated that I should grab onto Rob's arms and hold them behind the chair. Once my companion's arms were secured, Dr. Aid (and I am not making this up) crawled up onto his chest.

It was like I had died and awakened in an old W.C. Field's film.

With Dr. Aid placing her knees on Rob's chest and me pulling on his arms in order to increase his sleeve measurement, we managed to get one tooth out.

At that point, Rob decided that he did not need to have all of his wisdom teeth removed. In fact, he may have decided that he never wanted to have dental care again in his life. All I know for certain is that I was allowed to catch my breath and leave with my co-worker and first-ever dental patient.

I have physically recovered from my most recent dental adventures, but I think that, like Rob, my psyche may be permanently scarred. I find myself waking in the night with drool on my pillow, muttering "mucho gusto" to Susan. Fortunately, after 26 years in Latin America, Susan has learned to handle a lot.

"I have learned to use the word impossible with the greatest caution."

Wernher von Braun

Mission Impossible

I will get straight to the point.
I RECEIVED MY RESIDENCY VISA TODAY!
It is a true miracle. The man who was ahead of me in line today makes his living by helping people get their residencies. He asked me if I was married to a Costa Rican.

"No," I replied.

"Well, then," he assumed, "you must have a child who was born in Costa Rica, right?"

When I shook my head, he was astonished that I was about to receive my residency. I wasn't surprised, since I'd been told long ago that I was pursuing the impossible dream.

Today's wait in Immigration is another chapter of a long saga. I managed to choke back tears at a couple of points in the process today, but overall it was a much easier experience than last week's. It was shorter, too – only three and a half hours!

One has to wonder why it should take over three hours – especially considering I was supposed to only have to wait through the "firma" (signature) line today!

All told, I had to wait through five lines today. I hit the first one by 6:40 a.m., intentionally arriving early to secure a good position by the official opening time, 8:00 a.m. Today the lines were smaller and better organized than last week. Last week, some people set up tents and camped all weekend in the Immigration entrance just to be assured of a good position for Monday's appointments. Today I was grateful for Woody's brilliant idea to bring along a portable camp stool. I sat comfortably in line, a paperback book serving as my laptop desk while I wrote more than a dozen letters.

Last week many people called and complained to TV stations and newspapers after horrendous immigration experiences like my own. All week long, the Ministry of Immigration has had *lots* of bad press! They have had to clean up their act a little, hoping to convince the TV cameras to leave them alone.

My first line wasn't too discouraging. I was 20th in a line of about 100. When I hit the second line at the infamous "Puerta Dos" (door number two), I was third in position, and I felt a surge of hope. They didn't wait on us in order, but still, compared to last week, the wait was short. The third line at window four wasn't bad at all, and I figured I had it made when they had me actually sign my residency card. The official told me they would call me soon and hand me the final copy. I'd barely sat down again, when she came looking for me.

"You are missing one bank deposit."

No! It can't be! I've made four deposits already!

She insisted. This one was for $2.

"But," she said, "there is a bank right here, so it should be quick, and you can come right back to me for the final residency card."

I headed to find the bank window.

I couldn't believe my eyes. There were 50 people in the bank line!

I pulled out my camp stool again and began writing more letters. The line moved very slowly.

The deposit made, I headed back to window four, only to find that I could not speak to the official again without waiting through yet another line. (This is the point where I had to choke back the tears.)

I only got two more letters written before I was called. The official took my deposit slip and headed to the back to get my card. When she returned, she didn't hand me a card. Instead she addressed me with a stern reprimand.

"You were supposed to be here on the fifth of October! Why didn't you come?"

I swallowed hard before kindly replying that I had spent all day there on the 5th, only to be turned away and told to return today. It took some convincing, but she returned to her supervisor and finally got the authority to hand me the coveted card.

Apparently, my residency was granted a month ago. It is only valid for six months, so, technically that means it will expire in only five months. The last time I made an appointment, the first available spot was four months away. Does that mean I have to start this all over again in just a few weeks?!?

That thought tempers my rejoicing a bit. But as I sit today, observing my haggard facial expression on this coveted residency card, I am so thankful for this small "mission accomplished" and for all those who have faithfully prayed for me during this process.

By the way, when I got home I watched the local news on TV. Once again, the Ministry of Immigration made the news – and there I was, my back to the camera, perched on my campstool!

"You can never go home again, but the truth is you can never leave home, so it's all right."

Maya Angelou

Where Am I From?

I have been awake and hiding under the covers for the past hour ruminating on a deep, philosophical question. I am not embarrassed by this confession. When it is 16 below zero, anything that keeps you under multiple blankets is to be considered a positive thing.

The question that I have been struggling with is, "Where am I from?" As silly as this may sound, I get asked the question a lot in my travels and am more and more confused about how I should answer.

For most of you, this question is probably easy. Certainly it is going to be easier for many to answer than the alternative, "Where am I going?"

In some ways, I suppose the response to my own question should be easy enough for me.

WOODY AND SUSAN ROLAND

Lake City, Minnesota, is inked in my dog-eared passport like a tattoo. It is something which I have no more ability to change than the color of my eyes or hair – if I had any. Although Lake City is now being gentrified by money from Minneapolis, it is still a river town on the Mississippi. I was born looking out on a river that could take me to the rest of the world.

In some ways, it did.

There will always be something of Minnesota in me and about me. I genuinely believe that most children *are* above average. Wherever I am in the world, if given a chance to look at a U.S. newspaper, I will check to see how the Twins are doing. I am not surprised to see lime jello in the salad section of a buffet restaurant. I am not surprised by how large some of the folks are in the buffet line. However, I am surprised how they got *that* big eating lime jello!

My confusion concerning where I am from stems from the fact that I moved to Texas when I was still at an impressionable age. It changed me in a way that has never allowed me to go home again.

Although one of my seminal experiences in Texas occurred in 1972, I didn't actually move there to live until 1973. My father and mother drove me to Longview. When we said good-bye, they both cried. That was completely understandable for my mother. That is what mothers do. However, my father held Minne-

GOD SAVE THE EGGS!

sota stoicism as a high cultural value. Still, I think that he already knew I had accepted Texas as a state of mind and a worldview.

Now, when I say "Texas" I am not referring to that part of the state many of you are currently imagining. You cannot convince me West Texas is even really part of this world. In fact, it may be proof that Satan has run out of room in his current abode and is leasing additional properties.

"My Texas" is filled with southern pine forests, bass lakes and bluebells. It is a place of big dreams and bigger stories. It has better barbeque, richer ice cream and more "characters" than any other part of the world that I have seen, and I have seen a lot of it.

When Susan and I left Texas to prepare ourselves to serve as missionaries in Bolivia, it was one of the hardest things I had ever done. Somehow, I knew that I would never hear that kind of country music again.

Of course, there is additional confusion in my mind about where I am from because we did our preparation for Bolivia in Chicago. As things turned out, we ended up living several years in the city of big shoulders. To this day, when people in Latin America ask us, "Where are you from?" I will say, "Texas," while Susan responds, "Chicago."

We are a mixed marriage.

Chicago is Chicago. Until you have experienced Michigan Avenue in December and Lincoln Park in July, you will not understand that statement. Chicago is a special place in my mind. I say this even though (to borrow a phrase from Steve Goodman) the Cubs have turned me into a criminal. They have disappointed me again and again and again. However, there is always next year. Let's play two!

I have a daughter and son-in-law in Chicago. Krista has said that I can live with them when I am old. I'm not sure if she has discussed this with Chris. I'm not sure if I am ready to return to Chicago.

Most of my adult life has been spent in Latin America. I am no longer a novice. The surface warmth and charm wore off a long time ago. Still, it has changed me in ways that I can no longer explain.

For example, I have a hard time praying out loud in English – too many meals, church services and graduations where I have had to do it in Spanish. I have a hard time greeting people without hugging or kissing them. This can be difficult and awkward. My relatives in Minnesota don't understand why I keep trying to touch them.

Some of the things that so many people complain about regarding Latin America are the very things that endear it to me.

I take bureaucracy to be a full-contact sport. I think driving *should* be an adventure. Everyone needs to have a good, "I-have-to-run-to-the-bathroom" story. If you don't, I have several extra ones which I would be willing to give you for the right price.

All of this leaves me confused. Fortunately, I don't have too much time to worry. Susan tells me I have to pack my bags – I have another trip to make. Another country to visit – maybe another place to be from.

"Good decisions come from experience, and experience comes from bad decisions."

Author Unknown

The Allergist

One nice thing about Costa Rica is that as many as 2,000 species of plants may be found here.

However, that also means that there are about 2,000 varieties of pollens in Costa Rica. When we moved here, our youngest daughter, Kari, discovered that she was very allergic to at least a few of those.

After she suffered terribly despite taking every kind of medicine imaginable, I finally took the bull by the horns and got a referral for an allergist to see Kari. She is petrified of needles, but was so miserable that she decided it would be worth having the testing done in order to begin allergy shots. A physician friend of mine highly recommended an allergist in the capital city of San José.

I should have had a premonition when I

called to make an appointment.

"When would you like to come in?" the receptionist asked.

"Is there a chance we can get in tomorrow?"

"Sure, you name the time."

"Would 2 p.m. be OK?"

"Fine! We are in a building right across from the San Juan Hospital, on the third floor."

In blissful ignorance, I thought we were lucky to be able to get in the very next day at the time of our choice. Always be suspicious of a doctor with an empty appointment book.

The next day we found a parking spot in a not-too-pleasant area of the city. I already had my doubts about the San Juan Hospital, but still had great faith in my friend's referral. As we walked up to the building, we looked warily at one another. The outside of the building gave us the creeps.

We stepped inside and punched the button for the elevator. After clanking and groaning, a double cage door opened, revealing the interior of the elevator. It looked like it was capable of handling up to two people, weighing fifty pounds each. We again exchanged uncomfortable glances and opted for the stairs.

The stairs were a bit hard to find, since it was so dark inside. The wiring for the occasional light bulb was visible through the deteriorating wooden slatted walls. If ever I had seen a fire trap, this was it!

Upon arriving on the third floor, we didn't

have to look too hard for the allergist's office. There were only two other doors. We weren't sure whether to knock or step in. Gingerly we opened the door to the waiting area. There was a small desk with an antiquated phone and about six chairs inside. No people. No receptionist. Totally quiet.

"Upe!" I called. (Upe is a polite way in Costa Rica to say, "Is anyone home?") A door opened, and a man peered out. The embroidered name on his lab coat confirmed it was indeed the doctor in question. A cigarette dangled from his mouth as he told us to take a seat. He would be with us in just a moment.

We brushed the chairs off before sitting down. Stacked beside us were magazines from the 1980's. The windows were partially covered by thick, dust-coated drapes. The exhaust from the busy street outside poured in through the slatted windows, brown-tinged from the city smog. The doctor's degrees on the wall looked like pages ripped out of one of the original Sears catalogues.

We sat meditating on our fate for a few minutes before I firmly grasped Kari's hand and said, "We're out of here!!"

She hesitated, whispering loudly, "But, Mami! What about our appointment?"

We were half way down the stairs by that time. As we ran out of the building, I swear I saw a curtain pulled back on a third floor window. I'm quite sure that dust flew and cigarette ashes dropped from the doctor's astonished mouth. I am a registered nurse and the daughter of a nurse and doctor. I was taught to respect professionals and their opinions. Still, I never regretted my hasty decision. As Kevin Dyer, the founder of International Teams, used to say, "Make a decision and make it right."

Every step we took distancing ourselves from that office made our decision "righter and righter."

"When preparing to travel, lay out all your clothes and all your money. Then take half the clothes and twice the money."

Susan Heller

The Revenge of the Rupiah

I am sitting in the airport in Jakarta, Indonesia, and I am a defeated man.

By way of explanation, I should tell you that Susan always counts up the various national currencies in my pockets when I return from trips and places them in envelopes for me to use the next time I return to a particular country. Occasionally, she reminds me that I will probably not have a great need for this currency in the future. This quiet (and gentle) reminder has provoked in me the almost pathological desire to end my visits in a country with none of their currency in my pocket. Nothing. Zippo.

"Don't change money that you don't need." This is the traveling motto that I live by.

I traveled to Jakarta to visit with some International Teams workers. They have been doing a great job responding to the needs of those hurt in the recent tsunami. They are also beginning to build relationships with the hope of sharing Jesus with their new friends.

Since I was only going to be in Indonesia for a few days, I decided at the airport to get the equivalent of $50 US in local currency. I figured this would be enough to take my co-workers out for a nice meal or two and make sure that I could pay for all the taxis. It turns out that 50 dollars is worth about 500,000 Rupiah! I can assure you that in a country that still has coins worth less than 500, that is a pocketful of currency.

This morning I thought I was well-positioned to reach my goal. I had to take a taxi to the airport and still had 104,000 Rupiah burning a hole in my pocket. I knew the taxi would charge me somewhere around 100,000. I also knew that Susan was going to be proud of me. There would be almost nothing left to put in the dreaded Indonesia currency envelope.

Unfortunately, I had forgotten that in Indonesia the passenger pays for all the tolls while in a taxi. I have no idea if my driver was circling the airport or not, but I must have paid seven tolls en route. I was starting to sweat bullets – I didn't think that I would have enough for the fare.

Fortunately, the tolls, taxi and treasure (sorry, I have been listening to Chuck Swindoll sermons) all came together at a perfect moment, and I walked away from the driver with only 5,000 Rupiah in my pocket. This looked to be the beginning of a wonderful international trip.

Once inside the airport, I began to consider the possibility of sending one of my carry-on pieces as checked baggage. It occurred to me that this might save my back and also make the trip easier. The only problem was that this bag has no easy way to secure it. Fortunately, there was one of those places to get your suitcase covered in plastic sandwich wrap. When I asked the price he said, "25,000 Rupiah."

Have no fear. I still had 10 Singaporean dollars in my wallet. So, I changed them and received about 80,000 Rupiah. I was not concerned. I could always buy a soda. Besides, the Singapore envelope would now be empty as well. Yes, sir, this was shaping up to be a good day.

When I went to the check-in counter I was informed that I would have to pay a 100,000 Rupiah exit fee. If you are doing the math, you realize that I only had 60,000 in my pocket. This meant a return trip to the money changer where I found out that the smallest U.S. bill I could change was a $20. I walked away from the window holding almost 260,000 Rupiah!

I was beginning to feel desperate. The currency situation was slipping out of my control.

Having paid my exit fee, I went through immigration to the international side of the airport. The solution to my problem became obvious as I looked around the stores. I would do what people with too much disposable income (a very appropriate term for the infamous Rupiah) do throughout the world; I decided to buy a coffee at Starbucks.

Unfortunately, after ordering the largest coffee they produced AND a cinnamon roll, I STILL had 70,000 Rupiah. They were beginning to call the flight, and I was feeling desperate! I could almost hear Susan asking me when I planned my next trip to Indonesia.

Running to my gate, I spied a possible solution. A souvenir shop! Although I almost never buy this type of thing, I spotted something that I knew Susan would appreciate... a finger drum. Susan enjoys playing rhythm when I play guitar. This would be great. In my opinion, it HAD to cost more than 70,000 Rupiah.

To make a long story short, I am now in Singapore waiting for my flight to Hong Kong. I am walking around this elegant airport with a hand-carved Indonesian drum that I am not at all certain the U.S. customs folks will even allow into their country. My pockets are full of 1,000 Rupiah notes (the only change the fellow in Indonesia had available). I am hungry and have almost no Singaporean currency. I refuse to change any U.S. cash for fear that I will fill up the Singaporean envelope back in Costa Rica. All in all, the Euro is starting to make a lot of sense to me.

"Choosing what you want to do, and when to do it, is an act of creation."

Peter McWilliams

Juxtaposition

"**T**he act or an instance of juxtaposing or the state of being juxtaposed." [The American Heritage Dictionary of the English Language: Fourth Edition. 2000]

(Hmm... and my teachers used to complain about MY definitions!)

Transitive Verb: Juxtapose

"To place side by side, especially for comparison or contrast." [Ibid.]

That's more like it. My jet-lagged mind is a bit fuzzy about what the term "transitive verb" means, but at least I can understand the definition. Well, almost.

It seems like a lot of the parts that make up our lives can only be understood when we place them side by side with each other. The seeming contrast of those individual parts helps us to understand something more pro-

WOODY AND SUSAN ROLAND

found about who we are as a person.

Like you, my life is made up of a number of contrasts. Sometimes it is hard to reconcile those individual components.

I have just returned from Auckland, New Zealand, where I participated in what were meant to be my final Executive Team meetings with International Teams. I had asked last year to be relieved of these responsibilities so that I could concentrate on my role as Latin America Regional Director. I continue to count it a privilege to be a leader in this exciting ministry.

As usual, the meetings were challenging, interesting and looooong. I think we made excellent progress in directing the work of this dynamic missions community. Some good things are happening, and I believe the Lord will allow us to see even better things done for Him in the future.

Still, I ended the meetings weary of sitting in a room for five days with nine other human beings – as wonderful as those people are.

I admit it. I can be dangerous when I am weary of sitting in meetings. There is something about long meetings that brings out the 13-year-old boy that still lives somewhere in my 48-year-old body. The responsible missions leader becomes the kid sitting in the back of Spanish class, daydreaming and hoping the hour will end.

I rarely have the opportunity to look around the places I visit. Instead, I fly into a place, sit in meetings and fly back to Costa Rica. This time was going to be different. Some of our missions alumni from Bolivia live in Auckland, and I had made plans to spend a few days with them.

When Murray Wynn asked me what I would like to do while I was visiting with him, the "13-year-old" looked him straight in the eye and said, "I think I'd like to jump off the Skytower!"

Unfortunately, as I flew into the country on Quantas Airlines, I had viewed a fairly typical tourist video put together by some government ministry in New Zealand. In the video, they showed a clip of people "platform jumping" from the Skytower – 620 feet straight up in the air. This was unfortunate because it was the only thing that came to mind when Murray asked me what I wanted to do.

It is also unfortunate because there is still a lot of the 13-year-old boy in Murray's 60-year-old body. Once I had said it, it was almost impossible to back down.

The very next day, after a brief training seminar on the ground floor, I found myself in a jumpsuit and harness in the elevator going up the tallest structure in the Southern Hemisphere. The only way I can describe the sensations in my body is to say that I felt like I was about to visit one of those physicians that like to perform particularly nasty examinations on 48-year-old men.

The only person in the elevator with me was a woman who had also made the decision to jump. My only consolation is that she looked worse than I felt. I really thought she was going to pass out.

I like to believe that, even at this point, the 48-year-old man would have persuaded the 13-year-old boy to be sensible. However, when the elevator doors popped open (showing an incredible view of the Auckland Harbor), the two jumpmasters greeted us with the question, "All right! Who is going first today?"

My elevator companion yelped out, "He is!"

"Madam, I hardly know you."

One of them grabbed me by an arm and took me through a door where he hooked me up to a safety line (oxymoron?). Both of the jumpmasters checked my harness and various connectors one more time, and then it was through the door and onto the platform.

It was like walking the plank at 630 feet above the ocean!

Once I was on the platform, my jumpmaster told me to turn right. I managed to get my legs to disobey the few synapses still firing in my brain. The jumpmaster attached the "emergency line" (WHAT emergencies?!). Next, he attached the main line. Time was running out.

I was now instructed to turn left, which required extensive communication between my ears, my brain and those legs over which I was progressively losing control. A hand was placed on support wires on each side of the plank, er, platform. Some part of the brain registered they were my hands.

My jumpmaster (his name has been forever erased from my brain) now told me that he was going to count down from three, at which point I should jump. I felt like I was in a standard comic bit: "Excuse me. Do I jump on one or after one?" "I will count three, two, one and then say, Jump… that's when you go."

In some part of my receding consciousness, I noticed that he was edging away from me and the lip of the platform.

I hadn't been this alone since I had waited for the doctor to come into the examination room for my last physical. It was the same feeling I used to get while waiting outside the principal's office.

"Three, two, one… jump!"

The world stood still.

I jumped.

I didn't scream. I only felt like it.

I would like to tell you of all the amazing thoughts and sensations that I experienced falling belly first towards concrete (some macabre individual had painted it to resemble a target with a bulls-eye). I would like to tell you of the exultation and freedom that I experienced. I would like to… but, I can't. My brain had ceased functioning the minute I jumped off that platform.

A few of you will be glad to know that I survived with no pulled muscles or twisted ankles – to say nothing of not being atomized on the concrete target.

Those few of you who are glad will be disappointed to know what happened next.

Before going up in the elevator, I had

swapped stories and jokes with the jumpmaster down below. His name was Connor, and he was from Dublin. As the adrenaline rush began to ebb, Connor looked at me and said, "Woody, would you like to do it again? I can let you do it for free."

Yup. The 48-year-old man thinking about "deals like these" took the 13-year-old boy up the elevator again, and both of them jumped one more time.

In a way, it wasn't all that different from some of the decisions that I have to make as Latin America Regional Director. You try to make sure you have covered all the bases. You attempt to think of everything that could go wrong. However, after much prayer, sometimes you just have to move ahead and see how the Lord is going to work everything out.

Sometimes you have to jump.

I am back in Costa Rica once again. Susan has quit looking at me out of the corners of her eyes. However, she continues to make occasional groaning noises while she shakes her head. Hopefully, I will make some progress in that area in the coming week.

"I mean if you put all of your eggs in one bas-
ket, boy, and that thing blows up you've got a
real problem."

Jerry Bruckheimer

God Save the Eggs!

Picture yourself balanced precariously on
a small boat tied to a river bank by a
rope with twelve feet of slack. You've
carefully pulled the boat as close to the steep
steps as possible. You warily step onto the boat
to unload a large ice chest heavily loaded with
170 eggs. With one foot on the boat and one
on the river bank, you take care to not move
too quickly, hoping to sling the chest over the
side of the boat and land the precious cargo
safely on shore. As the chest touches the step,
of course the "panga" makes an equal and
opposite reaction (faithfully following Newton's
law), and you find one leg gently swinging out
into the river current. Unfortunately, you are not
made of rubber. Your other leg cannot pull you
safely to shore while holding the chest at the
same time.

WOODY AND SUSAN ROLAND

Dreamlike, you now see eggs slowly, steadily spilling into the river as you choke out the cry, "God, save the eggs!"

You've just pictured one of several adventures on my Sarapiqui River "medical" trip. Let me backtrack. One of our Costa Rican team mates, Donald, told me about a nurse who has a boat clinic to minister to medical needs among the poor that live along the Sarapiqui River. Longing for an opportunity to use my nursing skills, I worked to set up a two night trip to visit "Dr. Ana." I never really got to speak to her myself before the trip, but finally received indirect confirmation that the trip was on. Donald's family of four, Stephanie, and I would head out on Tuesday. (Stephanie is a team mate who has completed three years of medical training.)

I held my expectations loosely, since I had little idea of what was planned for us. My only hope was that Stephanie and I would have the opportunity to use our medical skills in some way to help the river community.

On Tuesday I drove our group over the mountains and through the Braulio Carillo National forest. We crossed heart of palm, pineapple and banana plantations to get to the hot river town of Puerto Viejo. From there we expected to take a two hour river taxi to the mission base.

As we awaited the boat, sweltering at the dock, a short, stout woman dressed in muddy boots, Goodwill shorts, a filthy tee-shirt and a ratty hat stepped up to me. In broken Spanish she asked, "Where are you going?" It ended up to be Dr. Ana herself! She totally ignored me when I tried to introduce her to Stephanie. Interrupting me, she asked, "Who is the lightest of you that is able to drive?"

That question rather threw me off. Did she mean for one of us to drive a boat?!?

She explained enigmatically, "My car is being repaired."

It became evident that she intended all but one of us to take the river taxi while the other was to drive her on errands and return with supplies loaded on the panga. Since Donald was the only other driver and he was gone at that moment, taking my car to a garage on the far side of town for safe-keeping, I volunteered to be her "light driver."

Rebecca, a strapping young American woman, towering over me in height and outweighing me by about 70 pounds, joined us, dressed in what was to be the typical attire for the next two days – muddy boots and a ratty hat. Ana stepped into the bank for money as I plied Rebecca with questions.

"How did you get here?" "What are we doing?" "Where is Ana's car?" "Am I supposed to go back and get my car?"

We began to walk to Ana's house on the other side of town. I ran into Donald as he was walking back to the pier to catch the river boat taxi. We were both sweating rivers with temps and humidity in the upper 90's. Rebecca and I arrived at Ana's house after a fifteen minute walk. I sat for a few minutes with a young Peruvian man named Anthony while Rebecca began to wash clothes. Anthony seemed mostly interested in sitting in front of the fan... a pastime that looked pretty inviting to me at the moment as well!

Ana was expecting me to pick her up from the bank in order to drive her on errands in my car. So, I left Rebecca and Anthony and headed back to the bank. I saw that Dr. Ana still had a long line ahead of her, so I decided to go pick up our portion of the cargo at the dock, knowing that the public boat would be taking off soon. (Their departure time had been delayed by an hour.) After loading the car, I sat outside the bank for another ten minutes, sweltering in the heat. Ana came out to inform me that there were still ten people ahead of her in line, so she sent me to go unload three things from the "panga" - a "boat bag," a lantern, and a box of eggs. She described her boat to me and where to find it, and then returned to the queue. She also mentioned, "We must leave by 4 p.m. at the latest." By now it was 1:30. "Plenty of time," I thought.

I found her boat with little difficulty and easily unloaded the bag and lantern. The chest of eggs you've already read about. As a result of that ordeal, I ended up stepping onto an underwater stair smashing my hand under the chest while trying to save the eggs. A huge blood blister on my hand was pulsing painfully.

GOD SAVE THE EGGS!

I felt sick about the broken and lost eggs, but I was thankful that I had managed to save at least 80% of them. I decided then and there that I would immediately tell Ana and apologize for the loss.

Ana took another 20 minutes in the bank, but finally came out. I confessed my egg mishap and asked her forgiveness. She looked at me in dismay and cried out, "Those eggs were supposed to pay for my car repairs!"

So much for forgiveness! Over the next day and a half I would hear no end of her disparaging comments about the lost eggs. She told everyone what a problem I had caused! (I learned later that the lost eggs were worth about $3... probably a fourth of what I spent on gas doing errands for her.)

For the next two hours I ran from one end of the city to another, often using my problem-solving and planning skills to help Ana and Rebecca get their list of errands taken care of. I got to know just about every street and store in town. I bought chicken feed, live chicks, gasoline, LP gas, rice, nails... you name it!

Throughout the afternoon I got to know Anthony a bit better. Ana would often use her broken Spanish to give him orders. When she walked away, I would ask Anthony if he understood what she wanted.

"Not a clue!" he would reply.

So, I would go back to Ana and try, often in vain, to get a more clear explanation in English.

Once she sent me off on errands and when

WOODY AND SUSAN ROLAND

I returned she gave me a hard time for not going to the boat to get an address book that she'd forgotten. She said, "That cost us at least 20 minutes!" (She had remembered the book just after I had already taken off with yet another list of errands. There was no way I could have known to bring that book!)

By now Rebecca had run out of Ana's money and we still had a significant list of supplies to buy from the supermarket. Also, she had told Anthony to divide up the chicken feed into smaller sacks so we wouldn't overload the boat. Of course, there were no extra sacks to divide the feed into. So, Anthony and Rebecca were totally stumped as to what to do. Ana was at the house on the phone now and did not want to be disturbed. It was already 4PM, so I decided to take the reins. I found two sacks for Anthony to begin dividing some of the feed. I drove Rebecca to the grocery store and told her to wait at the register until I got back with money. I drove back to the two feed stores, searching for extra feed bags.

Having failed on the feed bag expedition, I rejoined Anthony to improvise a way to divide out the 500 pounds of chicken feed I'd lugged to the house in my car. We put some in buckets and some in plastic bags. As we juggled the chicken food Anthony told me about Ana's latest boating venture. She'd overloaded that very same panga with goods and live chickens. When her passenger boarded, the weight was too much, so the front end went under and everyone and everything went overboard. River people dove in to help salvage people, goods, and most of the chickens. Eight chickens had disappeared, but thankfully no people had drowned.

Anthony went on to warn me, "This is too much weight once again. I'm not sure the boat can handle it." I somberly looked at our reduced load – 250 pounds of chicken feed, three passengers, no extra gas cans in order to save on weight, 50 live chicks, 50 pounds of rice, etc. The load loomed large and the sun was sinking lower. Just the night before I'd heard words of warning from a fellow teammate. "Ana is crazy, but don't worry, you'll be fine if you just remember one thing. Never, *never* go on the river at night with her!"

By 5 p.m. Ana and Rebecca seemed resigned to not complete all their errands and decided to head for the dock. They had no plan for how to get the three of us and a quarter ton of supplies to the panga and get my car back to the safety of the garage at the house on the opposite end of town. I suggested we take Anthony along to help load the boat and I would drive the car back, park it, and take a taxi back to the dock. Ana said the taxi would be too expensive: "It's only a fifteen minute walk."

Looking at my watch, I decided the $1.50 for a taxi was worth 15 more minutes of daylight. (Taxi fee = 15 eggs!)

WOODY AND SUSAN ROLAND

My heavy laden Suzuki groaned its way to the dock and we all proceeded to carry heavy sacks and buckets down to the panga. I left the three of them unsteadily adjusting the load. Meanwhile I hurried to get the car parked, contracting a taxi to follow me to her house to save me a bit more time.

When the taxi left me at the dock, it was 5:25 p.m. - 25 minutes until sunset! Ana and Rebecca were awaiting me, giving me careful warnings about how to step into the boat, with the hopes it wouldn't sink. Ana asked me just one question.

"Do you swim?"

My reply was, "Yes, I do, but quite honestly I prefer not to."

My mind was whirring. I was seriously, seriously debating staying behind and simply sending word to the rest of my team that I would join them the next day, taking the river taxi during daylight hours. I was desperately praying for wisdom. There were no bells or shouts from heaven, so I gulped down my fears, uttered a final prayer of trust and stepped gingerly into the small gap left strategically for my body.

The panga wavered with indecision, "Should I sink now or later?!?"

We made several quick adjustments of weight: "Susan! Put your right foot ahead on that chicken feed sack! Susan! Put your left leg ahead on the other sack! Susan! Lean your left arm way behind on the rice sack! Don't smash the chicks right behind you! Hold onto the chick box, it's not secure! Keep your eyes ahead! Watch for logs and stumps!"

I resigned myself to a two hour game of Panga Twister.

Left foot – green! Right hand – red! Right foot – yellow!

For the next two hours I never once was able to sit upright with my feet in front of me. My back was one big, hopeless kink. As the last traces of light faded from the sky, my eyes were as strained as my back, looking for shapes that would signal a sure sinking. Often my heart would race as a shape leapt into view right in front of the boat, proving only to be a mass of harmless bubbles.

Rebecca asked if I might have a flashlight. Sure I did! But, it was in my bag which had gone up river with the taxi. She replied, "Oh, well! You can't really see much better with a flashlight."

The trip seemed endless. Often the motor would get tangled with weeds and Ana would shout to lean back as she revved the motor out of the water. The river would lap over the front end, like a tiger running his tongue over his teeth.

Well after dark I spotted a few lights along the river bank. "I think that's the town of Arbolitos. We are only ten minutes away!" cried Ana.

Five minutes later my hopes were deflated once again.

WOODY AND SUSAN ROLAND

"No, that wasn't the town yet. We must be further away than I thought."

After what seemed like hours, I finally spotted a flashlight sweeping across the trees, high above the bank. "That's it!" shouted Ana and Rebecca.

We all yelled to the people on shore, "Bring the flashlights!" as Ana swung the boat towards the invisible bank. Several more lights appeared.

As "helpers" are wont to do, they all shined the lights directly into our faces, blinding us more than ever.

We continually shouted in Spanish and English, "NO! Point the flashlights down! Abajo! Abajo!" Occasionally the light would glance over the steep steps on the bank, briefly showing that we were veering dangerously close to a blind collision. Just before hitting, our helpers got the idea, and suddenly the blessed stairs were in clear view as we bumped up against the lowest step.

I have never, ever been so happy to step ashore.

(Well, I take that back. The time I nearly drowned in the ocean, I happily fainted when I finally was able to step on the beach.)

I managed to shake the cramps out of my legs and climb up the steep stairs as the gang unloaded the panga. My teammates had been terribly worried. Maybe they should have been *more* worried than they *were*, truth be told! They had no clue of the horror of the past two hours on the dark, dangerous river.

I would not fully see my surroundings until the next morning. The station had only two 15 watt bulbs – one dimly lighting the dining area and the other in our bunkroom.

We ate a late supper by candlelight and soon afterwards retired to the bunkroom. Stephanie and I exchanged whispered stories. She told me that their trip was delayed several times, but was otherwise uneventful. Upon their arrival they'd had a lovely time chatting with Ana's "missionary interns." About six young women were living there, studying missions and working at the small farm that helps sustain the Palmas De Mamré mission.

I shared my experiences and we both tried to sleep. The bunk room we shared with one other woman was built with rough boards. The rustic bunks had two-inch thick foam mattresses. Though the conditions were very basic, we were comfortable enough. However, the unsettling events of the day left us both with a sense of spiritual oppression. Neither of us slept well.

We'd been warned that Ana calls for all to rise and shine before dawn. Sure enough, at 4 a.m. Ana began talking loudly in the room next door. By 4:30 we were gathered in the open dining area for a time of prayer before chores. As the sun's rays filtered through the river foliage, the beauty of the surroundings unfolded before my eyes.

By 5 a.m. I was helping feed and water the

chicks we'd brought as well as the other farm animals, including pigs. Everybody participated in the morning chores.

For the sake of time, I will skip most of my actual experience while at the river mission. Right after breakfast Stephanie and I were put to work in the primitive kitchen, washing dishes. Stephanie was also made responsible for the water pot set to boil in order to pluck the five chickens they were preparing to butcher and sell.

Ana talked at length with me. It became evident that there was no medical ministry taking place at this time. Not only that, it became clear that Ana had no professional healthcare training. (She'd worked in the US with child protection, supervision of a welfare office, and, most recently, selling real estate.)

My day was filled with two activities: 1) Washing dishes and cooking and 2) listening to Ana explain her vision for ministry. Our only "medical" activity came about when Rebecca came to Ana saying, "I have a palm thorn in my leg." Ana pulled out a needle and proceeded to poke around her muddy leg. (I hadn't seen Ana wash her hands once since my arrival.) After getting the thorn out, Ana proceeded to use the same dirty needle to probe several other spots on Rebecca's legs and feet. Inside I was screaming, "Let me out! Let me out!" But, I managed to keep my cool, reminding myself that someday this all would make a good story.

GOD SAVE THE EGGS!

As Stephanie, Donald's family, and I got on the early morning river taxi to head home after our two days at the station, I enjoyed the daylight version of the river trip. Every single tree trunk we skirted gave me one more opportunity to thank God for sparing my life on the Sarapiqui River.

"Blues is easy to play, but hard to feel."
Jimi Hendrix

Moaning Guitars

I am not sure what we do with the silence of God. Books have been written about it. Pictures have been painted expressing the emotions. Poems have been penned trying to describe its reality.

To my knowledge, nothing seems to fully connect with my own experience.

When God is silent, He seems exceptionally silent.

I have learned to be rather quiet about certain parts of my journey. People like to hear my funny stories. They seem to get something useful from my rather quirky exegesis. At least they humor me by saying that it is worthwhile.

At this point in our lives, Susan and I have been in vocational Christian ministry for 27 years. For 19 of those years, Susan has dealt with almost continual nausea, pain or some combination of both. For a number of years, we spent our visits in the States trying to find some solution. Several times we thought we had found it. Sometimes, Susan actually had some temporary relief.

God's silence always seemed the coldest when the symptoms appeared once again.

I cannot remember how many times I have sat by her side while she struggled to wake up from the anesthesia given to her while the doctors performed some procedure or surgery. That wouldn't be so bad, but Susan detests the experience of being even slightly intoxicated or drugged. At those times, I wished we could change places.

I seem to have more talent in that area.

I have no idea how much of our financial resources have gone to pay medical bills, prescriptions and inflated insurance premiums. It is probably best for me to remain ignorant.

One of the only things that provides comfort for me is the transparency of others who have sat listening to the silence. I imagine this is why I enjoy authors like Henri Nouwen, Fredrick Buechner and Philip Yancey. I would take more comfort from certain biographies, but those that overtly claim to be Christian are rarely honest. It is interesting that one of the few honest biographies or autobiographies is actually a diary published in the mid-1700's. David Brainerd's journals have remained in print for over 250 years. I would think that some Christian publishing houses would take notice.

GOD SAVE THE EGGS!

On Thursday, November 4, 1743, Brainerd penned these words: "Tis distressing to feel in my soul that hell of corruption which still remains in me." Many times his emotional pain was so intense that he felt cut off from the presence of God. January 23, 1743: "Scarce ever felt myself so unfit to exist, as now: I saw I was not worthy of a place among the Indians, where I am going ... None knows, but those that feel it, what the soul endures that is sensibly shut out from the presence of God: Alas, 'tis more bitter than death!"

Hardly the stuff of a Gospel of wealth and prosperity!

One author has counted at least 22 places in the diary where Brainerd longed for death as a freedom from his misery. For example, Sunday, February 3, 1745: "My soul remembers 'the wormwood and the gall' (I might almost say hell) of Friday last; and I was greatly afraid I should be obliged again to drink of that 'cup of trembling', which was inconceivably more bitter than death, and made me long for the grave more, unspeakably more, than for hid treasures." Sunday, December 16, 1744: "Was so overwhelmed with dejection that I knew not how to live: I longed for death exceedingly: My soul was 'sunk in deep waters,' and 'the floods' were ready to 'drown me': I was so much oppressed that my soul was in a kind of horror."

On second thought, maybe Christianity at the beginning of the 21st century is no longer capable of this type of honesty. It is strong medicine.

Brainerd suffered all of his adult life from sickness.

Now and again he would write something like, "In the afternoon my pain increased exceedingly; and was obliged to betake myself to bed ... Was sometimes almost bereaved of the exercise of my reason by the extremity of pain." In August of 1746 he wrote, "Having lain in cold sweat all night, I coughed much bloody matter this morning, and was under great disorder of body, and not a little melancholy." In September he wrote, "Exercised with a violent cough and a considerable fever; had no appetite to any kind of food; and frequently brought up what I ate, as soon as it was down; and oftentimes had little rest in my bed, by reason of pains in my breast and back: was able, however, to rode [sic] over to my people, about two miles, every day, and take some care of those who were then at work upon a small house for me to reside in amongst the Indians."

If my memory serves me correctly, Brainerd died at 29 years of age. From a ministry standpoint, he was a failure. His work was not lasting. He left no church and only a few disciples. However, "being dead he still speaks."

All of what I have written to this point would simply be a morbid exercise or a trip to the pity pot if it weren't for the reality of singing the blues.

GOD SAVE THE EGGS!

I need to make a confession here. I enjoy the blues. It makes no difference if it is Stevie Ray Vaughn, Robert Johnson or Eric Clapton. When some of their pain comes out in their guitars, it seems to take some of mine away.

This shouldn't be surprising.

The Psalms are filled with lamentations, prayers that were used in the worship of the temple to pour out the sorrows of Israel before God: "Out of the depths have I cried unto thee, O LORD. Lord, hear my voice: let thine ears be attentive to the voice of my supplications" (Psalm 130:1-2, KJV).

A psalm which many Christians have committed to memory and have made part of their prayers day after day is Psalm 51: 1-2 (KJV): "Have mercy upon me, O God, according to thy lovingkindness; according unto the multitude of thy tender mercies blot out my transgressions. Wash me thoroughly from mine iniquity, and cleanse me from my sin."

This prayer of confession has been prayed by the Church for centuries. Sometimes it has been sung to a melody. Sometimes it has been read as a responsive reading. Maybe it should have been a blues song.

Even Jesus cried before God.

It is He who should be the example of real Christian prayer. When He offered himself up on the cross He prayed: "My God, my God, why hast thou forsaken me?"

It sounds a bit like David Brainerd. It sounds

a bit like any other servant of God who has faced the dark night of the soul. It sounds like Stevie Ray Vaughn! Someone has said that singing the blues in church is a matter of honesty. Many of us come to church with a big load of troubles. We want to lay them down in God's presence, spread them out in God's sight and know that He takes them up and sometimes does away with them. We need to be open about our sins, open about our problems, open about our pain.

Sometimes we need to hear that ol' guitar moan.

"A sister smiles when one tells one's stories - for she knows where the decoration has been added."

Chris Montaigne

What I Learned From My Sisters

Susan and I drove across the Central Valley on Friday evening to participate in a new couples' ministry at our church, Principe de Paz. Driving on Friday in San Jose, Costa Rica, is never fun. Driving on Friday in December is the worst. Every year I tell myself I will not leave home in December until after Christmas. Every year I make the same mistake.

During the course of an interesting discussion with the other couples on the foundations of a healthy marriage, THE topic came up. You all know what I mean – toilet seat covers and the position in which men leave them. I always find the passion behind this issue to be particularly interesting. While I was listening to some bitter, recriminatory statements in the group, Susan leaned over and whispered in my ear, "Your sisters taught you well!"

WOODY AND SUSAN ROLAND

In that brief moment, I experienced an epiphany. The reason that Susan and I never struggled over this particular issue was not my innate male sensitivity, but the fact that my sisters taught me well. Considering the amount of emotion expended on the subject, I think I should be very grateful for their influence on my life.

As my mind began to wander (and my mind wanders all the time in meetings... even if I am the one preaching!), I began to think about other things that Janet and Joanne had taught me in life. It was amazing how fast the list began to grow.

"It is not socially correct to bite people when you disagree with them."

Because I was the youngest in my family and, at least for several years, the least erudite, I developed the habit of biting my siblings to help sway the argument in my direction. Through patient explanation (and beatings) by my sisters, I learned the futility of this communication technique. It is amazing how few Christian leaders have learned this lesson. They can be vicious. My only thought is they must not have had older sisters.

"Not everything that smells bad is bad."

Do you remember "Home Permanents?"

GOD SAVE THE EGGS!

The smell was overpowering. I can remember searching out the remotest corner of the basement on Saturday evenings trying to avoid that pungent and probably toxic odor. It was no use, there was no escaping it. Still, when the odor cleared and I recovered consciousness, the results were amazing. My sisters went from being my sisters to rather attractive young ladies. Learning to put up with the "stinky" in order to get to the good is a great ministry lesson that has served me well.

"Read faster, dummy!"

It is popularly believed in pedagogy today that negative stimulation does not work. This is not always true. After the first grade (when I was in the Bluebird, or, mentally incompetent reading group), my father decided that I should read aloud from the Bible for family devotions. Unfortunately, we only read from the King James Version in those days. The combination of my reading skills and the old English produced marathon family devotion sessions. My sisters (and I distinctly remember my brother, Harlan, also participating in this) provided levels of negative stimulation after we left the table that did wonders to my reading skills. I should be very thankful, and I will be, as soon as the knots on my head fully disappear!

WOODY AND SUSAN ROLAND

"Solvent is required to get oil paint out of hair."

I am not prepared to go into this learning episode right now, as I have a feeling it is still a sensitive subject for some people.

All in all, I am thankful for the preparation for life that my sisters provided me. If nothing else, it has apparently helped me avoid one of the most emotional marital struggles. This is not to say that Harlan did not also prepare me for life and ministry. However, "Techniques for Stretching Halloween Candy until April" probably deserves its own PowerPoint™ presentation.

"Hard choices are clear and easy when you don't have to make them."

Anne Plant

Some Choice!

S ometimes the best thing is to do is the hardest thing.

They attempt to teach us that truth when we are still children. However, for some of us (and I am NOT naming names here) it takes a while to sink in.

During the past couple of weeks, I have been reading in Jeremiah and Ezekiel. My brother-in-law, Vito, encouraged a number of us to read through the Chronological Bible this year. Unfortunately, from my perspective, all Bible reading programs eventually lead to Ezekiel. The combination of "Jeremiah with a thick slice of Ezekiel on top" can best be described as tough... especially if you add in a few detailed genealogy lists for spice.

But, as I said, sometimes you need to do the hard things.

WOODY AND SUSAN ROLAND

The other day, I came across these words while reading in Jeremiah: "Then I told them that the LORD had said: People of Jerusalem, I, the LORD, give you the choice of life or death. The Babylonian army has surrounded Jerusalem, so if you want to live, you must go out and surrender to them. But if you want to die because of hunger, disease, or war, then stay here in the city." (Jeremiah 21:8,9)

Can you imagine? A number of the "best and brightest" (including Ezekiel) have already been taken captive by the Babylonians. Most of these people in Jerusalem would have seen that terrible sight. They would still have some natural questions about what happened to those people taken from their home country in the most humiliating way possible. Now, they are offered the option of also being taken into captivity or dying in Jerusalem.

Some choice!

Still, what must have seemed like the worse choice to them really was the best. God did bring those people who chose to go into captivity through to the other side. In fact, He re-established Israel with them. It would seem that God is as good as His Word.

Go figure.

I am not sure what choices you are facing right now, or, what decisions you must make. I do pray that all of us who are serious about following Him will be willing to trust Him – even in the hard things.

"I'm not afraid of death. It's the stake one puts up in order to play the game of life."
Jean Giraudoux

Never Die Young, Never Grow Old

I received news today that an old acquaintance of mine is dying. I have not seen Karen for 33 years. In my mind she is still a beautiful, 19-year-old – off to try and save the world.

Apparently reality is once again different from my perspective.

The old adage says if you want to live you have to die. Of course, old adages sound better if you have a real chance at living long enough to put them in practice.

I am aware that dying is part of our lives. From where I sit, it seems my parents' main social outlet is attending the funerals of their friends. A few years ago I asked my mother not to send me the obituaries of everyone who has "passed." I think I may have offended her. Close friends have died, and I haven't heard a thing. You don't have to be older to have death be part of who you are.

One of the formative experiences of my youth was the death of my friend, Steve. Although Steve and I met through some kind of church activity, we both imbibed heavily in what has come to be known as the "60's." I remember returning home from a trip and my father telling me I should watch the news. The reporter said Steve's body had been found in a small river and police were investigating. I knew it had to be drug-related, and it was.

One day we had both been alive, talking about philosophy, politics and music. A few days later I was standing next to Steve's coffin.

It didn't seem right.

I have thought of Steve a number of times over the years. I have also visited his gravesite. Every time I go there the marker tells the same story: "Died, September 3, 1970."

I think of everything that I have done since 1970 and realize that Steve never had a chance to experience real life.

In 1971 I became a Christian. I married Susan in 1975. On May 10, 1978, we landed in La Paz, Bolivia, and began an adventure that has still not ended. Krista was born in 1979. Norma came to us in 1983 and, not long after that, Kari arrived.

Over all those years I have ministered in 46 countries and visited a few more.

Of course it hasn't all been good.

I remember riding on the back of a motor-cycle in Bolivia with bullets flying around me. I believe my prayer that morning was one of the most profound and sincere ones I have ever uttered. "Small butt. Small butt. Make it small, God."

He did.

I have been sick with enough diseases that Red Cross volunteers laugh at me when I offer to donate blood. All of those sicknesses have made me happy for each day I am alive. They also make me very respectful of the process of dying. It takes real courage to do it right.

Jesus likened the experience of being His disciple with dying. In Luke 14:25, 26, and 33 we read the following:

"Large crowds were walking along with Jesus, when he turned and said: 'You cannot be my disciple, unless you love me more than you love your father and mother, your wife and children, and your brothers and sisters. You cannot come with me unless you love me more than you love your own life. You cannot be my disciple unless you carry your own cross and come with me... So then, you cannot be my disciple unless you give away everything you own."

Sometimes old adages are right. They are just hard to live out in what we call life.

"I think that's really what the message this week of Easter is, that God can bring good out of bad. That he turns crucifixions into resurrections."

Rick Warren

It Could Be Worse

People in the Midwest are great at coming up with idiomatic expressions to explain the difficult. I am not sure, but I think that it might originate with being forced to live through long stretches of winter.

When the snow continues to fall in April, you can hear a native Minnesotan say, "Well, it could be worse."

I am sure that it could be worse, but I am not sure if I would like to be there for it. Even if it was worse and you actually survived, would that mean that you should defend such an existence?

Even asking such questions proves that I have been away too long. Without a doubt, I have become "soft"– a state of being that lesser souls (like those who winter in Florida,

WOODY AND SUSAN ROLAND

Texas or Arizona) suffer in secret shame. "Soft people" do not understand deeper theology.

I remember another expression that I often heard as I grew up. When something terrible happened in my life, Mother would say, "Well, you have to look for the good in the bad." I would often hear these words in situations as when a huge blemish erupted on my face before an important date.

Woody: "Ahh! One of the horns of the beast of Daniel has erupted on my forehead! I can't take Susan to the school play like this."

Mother: "Well, you have to look for the good in the bad."

Like I say, it is hard to defend such an existence.

A few months ago, we were confronted with a bad situation.

Nena, the country woman that Susan had the privilege to lead to the Lord last year, called our house on a Sunday morning. After our normal greetings, I told Nena that I would find Susan. Nena replied, "No, Mr. Woody. I called this morning so that Rodrigo could talk with you. We found out that our daughter is pregnant and my husband is very angry. I am not sure what he is going to do."

Rodrigo came on the line and began to share with me some of his feelings. I won't go into the details, but I was briefly concerned for the physical well-being of the young man in question. I will say that I had the privilege of praying on the phone with Rodrigo and then later in the week with him in person.

As the family adjusted to the bad situation, they decided they would allow the couple to get married. In fact, as a result of our conversations, Rodrigo became convinced that he needed to invest in the life of this young man. It was exciting to see the change in his perspective.

The family decided they would ask the local priest to officiate at the wedding ceremony. However, he refused and suggested the couple should just live together to see if the relationship would work out. I seriously doubt he passed this alternative on to anyone in Rome.

Rodrigo became upset enough that he decided the couple would have an "evangelico" ceremony and that Mr. Woody would perform it. "Mr. Woody" had his doubts about performing the ceremony, but it was hard to say "no" after telling Rodrigo of the importance of loving his daughter without any conditions.

Before the day of the wedding, Susan and I had the privilege of inviting the young couple to our cabin for supper and an evening of conversation. During the course of the evening, we also had the privilege of sharing the Gospel with them. We continue to pray this message will take root in their lives.

While I have performed a number of weddings in Latin America, I have never performed one for a group of country people in Costa

WOODY AND SUSAN ROLAND

Rica. I don't mind saying that it was a real challenge to try to understand some of their expectations.

Of course, since there is no evangelical Christian church in this area of Costa Rica, it was also hard for the folks to understand me. A few of them kept referring to me as "Father" and making reference to Susan as "the priest's wife." I doubt if we are going to inform Rome of this one, either.

Many of the people in the community told Rodrigo and Nena that it was wrong to have a Christian ceremony for their daughter. Rodrigo stood up to the pressure and insisted that we move ahead with wedding.

The actual wedding day was great. It took place on a hillside overlooking a scenic valley filled with coffee fields. There were just enough clouds to help keep the brilliant sun from burning my bald head.

Although Susan and I didn't know it, we had also signed on to help dress the bride's mother and father and the groom. It seemed that in this country community, there were few people who could understand the mysteries of tying a tie.

As I walked in before the assembled group of 150, it was a surprise for me to find several of our neighbors from around our cabin at the wedding. We have prayed that the Lord would allow us to share more openly with some of them. This seemed to be about as open as we could hope.

GOD SAVE THE EGGS!

I won't go into all of it, but I will tell you that the Lord seemed to be at work in that community. I felt great freedom in sharing the Gospel as the basis for success in marriage.

I have rarely had a "congregation" hang on my words in that way. As part of the service, Susan prayed for the couple. Several people were visibly moved.

Afterwards, we were invited to stay for a typical, Costa Rican campesino reception. The food was great, the music "rhythmic" and the conversations easy.

I ended the evening talking to one of the community leaders, the grandfather of the bride.

During the course of our conversation, he said, "You are easy to talk with. It is a very good thing that we are doing this together." These were strong words from a man who had resisted the idea of me being involved in the wedding.

Since we had developed such a rapport, I decided I would ask him for the secrets of wisdom that he had accumulated working the fertile land of Costa Rica. So, crouching on a rough–hewn, wooden bench in my best suit, I asked this wizened old man to share his thoughts on life with me.

The single light bulb illuminating us in the midst of the coffee fields and trees sparkled in his eye that night. He quickly responded, "Don Woody, there are three things that you have to remember in life. First, always make sure that you have a good sombrero and never leave home without it. Second, buy good boots. Third, always carry a big knife."

With the third statement he quickly drew a quality, seven inch knife from the back of his belt.

I must admit he didn't seem as peaceful as the Indian guru that many ask about the meaning of life. However, it is difficult to argue with a man with a drawn knife.

Susan has had a few conversations with Nena since the wedding. Apparently the people in the community were very moved by the whole ceremony. When Nena told Susan that she would have to come and share more with her neighbors, Susan was able to talk to Nena about her own responsibility to share the Gospel with her friends. Nena asked Susan, "You mean I can share this message, too?" "Yes, Nena. And you will be able to share it better than I can with your friends and relatives."

It is not easy for a young couple to start out under these circumstances. However, sometimes you have to look for the good in the bad.

Sometimes you don't have to look for it. Sometimes the good finds you in a coffee grove in Costa Rica.

"It's not hard to make decisions when you know what your values are."

Roy Disney

The Slingshot

Most of us have heard the expression "what goes up must come down." In my recent visit to the Gold Coast in Queensland, I had the privilege of proving the opposite true – what goes down must go up.

Well, at least what goes down *can* go up.

I spent the last part of August "down under" in Australia. Over two years ago, I received an invitation to speak at a student missions conference called *Reachout* in Katoomba, New South Wales. Because I was making the trip, International Teams asked me to extend my time and speak at several churches, colleges and seminaries.

I met my "minder" at the Brisbane airport after traveling 32 hours from San Jose. Rick Sirico is the Director of Mobilization for International Teams Australia. He was given the task of spending over two weeks with me to make sure I didn't needlessly embarrass the organization in my public appearances.

Obviously, Rick is a patron of lost causes.

After I had preached in four or five churches and fellowships, Rick arranged a day for me to meet with church leaders on the Gold Coast... one of the more affluent cities in Australia. On the way to my third meeting of the day, he drove me past an area known for its "adrenaline attractions" - bungee jumping, extreme amusements, and, most importantly (from my perspective), "The Slingshot."

At this point I would like to point out that Mr. Sirico has known me for several years. He is fully aware of my weaknesses... well, at least several of them. He knew there are limits to my ability to resist certain temptations. In other words, I am not responsible for what happened in the next few minutes.

Rick stopped the car and Grant Gerhke, an IT missionary who was spending the day with us, stepped out with me. We looked up at "The Slingshot," an apparatus built with the sole purpose of launching people into the sky at over 100 miles per hour. Willing (and unwilling) participants pull six "G's" as they go up over 240 feet in the air. Of course, once they are up, they do come down. Fortunately, the bungee cables allow the trip down to be somewhat ameliorated before the subjects come into direct contact with the ground.

When I looked at the Slingshot, I knew that I

was going to do it. My only question was whether I could get anyone else to do it with me.

I looked at Grant and thought I had my pigeon, er, companion.

"Grant, if I pay for it, will you go with me?"

"No, I don't think so."

"Come on! We'll be fine. Give it a try."

"No, I don't think that my wife would like it."

Here is where my "Minnesota Nice" came into play. People raised in rural Minnesota know they must always invite people three times... even if they have already been refused twice.

"Come on Grant. It will be fun. You won't get another chance."

"No...well, okay. I'll do it."

I won't bore you with the details. It was incredible. Going up was a literal rush. Looking down at the ground from our apex was mind numbing. Bouncing back and forth on the bungee was, well, bouncy.

As we were lowered down to the ground, the young lady in charge of the slingshot said, "If you do it again without getting out of your harness, we will let you do it for only $10.00." I told Grant that it was his call. This time he didn't hesitate and said, "Let's go." Boy, did we! If anything, the second time was more incredible than the first.

I should point out that the Slingshot of the Gold Coast was not the biggest thrill of my trip to Australia. To hear about my biggest adventure, I have to take you down to the Blue Mountains, west of Sydney.

I arrived in Katoomba with the other International Teams people to speak at the missions representatives' retreat – a gathering of missions leaders in Australia held every year immediately before Reachout. Though I did speak to the group, most of my time was spent making friends with some of these great men and women.

One lady looked me in the eyes at mealtime and asked me, "Are you nervous?" "No, why would I be nervous?" "You are responsible to give the invitation on Saturday evening at Reachout. All of the responsibility rests on your shoulders." I laughed and responded, "No. I think that God is responsible for the invitation. I just need to share his Word." She continued to stare me in the eye and said, "We take this very seriously here. This is the biggest event of our year."

Whoa! Somebody needs to get out more. Maybe try the Slingshot.

Still, she did make me think of my responsibility.

On Friday I spoke from Hebrews 11. It was encouraging that the Australians understood my sense of humor. Well, at least they were polite enough to laugh at my stories.

On Saturday I gave three seminars on youth ministry in Latin America. Standing room only. Rick Sirico was a great help. My voice was starting to fade.

Before speaking on Saturday evening, I had 15 minutes to look at my notes and pray. I have to admit that lady's comments about my responsibility were beginning to weigh on my mind.

Besides praying, I knew this type of pressure would require something extra. That's right; I decided to wear my special "Woody Woodpecker" cap given to me by one of our long-time friends and supporters. I actually began my sermon on Hebrews 12:1, 2 by telling why the hat meant so much to me.

At the end of the message, I gave a simple invitation to the participants at Reachout to dedicate themselves to cross-cultural ministry... to make disciples in the world. There was no music; no singing of "Just As I Am"; no manipulation – I hope. With my head bowed and my eyes closed, I had no idea of what kind of response there was to the invitation. After praying for a few minutes, I opened my eyes to see the entire front of the conference center filled with people; so many people that the organizers of Reachout did not have enough response forms and information packets ready for them.

There is no doubt that trying out the Slingshot was fun. However, preaching at Reachout was one of the most exciting things that I have done in years. There is nothing which compares to the knowledge that God has used us to touch other people's lives. Nothing.

As the meeting ended I had the privilege

of talking with and praying for several who had come forward. I know that many will experience ups and downs on their way to cross-cultural ministry. However, I also believe that God will use them for years to come.

"It's like driving a car at night. You never see further than your headlights, but you can make the whole trip that way."

E. L. Doctorow

Driving With Friends

I failed my first driving test.

At the time, I sensed that it was one of the worse failures of my life. Looking back, I haven't experienced much that would modify that early opinion.

I am still tempted to make excuses for myself. I had lots of experience driving by the time I took my test. I usually drove 20 miles illegally each day to get to driver's education!

Our teacher had asked me to take the test before any of the other fellows in my class. He mistakenly thought that I would easily pass and inspire confidence in some of the boys who only had more legitimate experience for their age.

Unfortunately, I was used to the "real world," and the driving range on which they gave the practical exam was anything but real. Long and short: I blew a stop sign and immediately failed.

A few weeks later I went back to re-take the test. Driving my father's 1964 Catalina, I was ready for anything. When I saw the black skid marks on the clean, white pavement of the driving range, I knew what was coming. So, when the State Trooper giving the exam started to say, "St...," I was already braking.

Unfortunately, my mother had placed a can of those pastel-colored dinner mints that were so popular in those years on the back window ledge. I will never forget that state trooper cleaning the brightly colored candies off of his regulation D.I. hat. You will be proud to know that I managed to keep a straight face.

Without a doubt, the best part about that day was going to my friend's house immediately after passing my test to go "cruising." I am talking about "windows down, music blaring, bare arm hanging out at just the right angle" cruising. Eyes always moving, looking for the girls that we were sure would be overcome by our "I-am-not-sure-what." Without a doubt Joe, Gary and I were going to conquer the world.

I was probably more alive that day than I have been at almost any other moment since.

A few weeks ago, I had the privilege of visiting with the same two men – now, not so young – with whom I went cruising on that memorable day. Joe needed to check out the location of a possible job site. So, at about 9:00 in the evening, I found myself in the back seat of a 900 Turbo Saab, with the music playing loud. This time Gary was at the wheel.

Driving down the road, listening to Larry Norman on the stereo, talking about things that were important to us, it was easy to imagine myself back in another time, another place, maybe even another planet.

Last week, I was on yet another trip. No, not *that* kind of trip! This one took me to Texas and Louisiana. While visiting with some dear friends in Texas, once again I found myself in the back seat of a car. This time it was a convertible. Seated next to me was Jack Faulkner, a friend who knew me when I still had hair. We were on our way to buy the "best hamburger around" at the Brenham airport. The last time I rode with Jack in a convertible, we were in a yellow, Volkswagen bug. By this I mean a "real bug" with a four cylinder, air-cooled engine. This was back when we had all the major problems in the world solved.

It's a pity the politicians didn't listen to us!

Although the wind could no longer blow back my hair, it was still nostalgic to feel it whipping past me as we drove by fields filled with bluebonnets and primroses. It felt like 1973, and, amazingly enough, the girl that I dated way back then was the same one I found myself looking at now. At least she has enough hair to merit the term "windblown." She is still beautiful, and I would marry her all over again if I could.

Jack, Karen, Susan and I are all parents of married kids. However, for a few minutes as we drove down that road, I was able to feel like a teenager again. I was in a convertible with precious friends and the woman of my dreams.

It may seem strange that I am writing about these things on an Easter Sunday. There are probably more profound subjects upon which I should touch.

Still, there is something about the old stories and the old friends that give me special comfort.

I became a Christian in the fall of 1971. Back in those days, I thought that Jesus was the dearest, most alive friend that I would ever have. I believed that He really got up out of that tomb just to save guys like me. I didn't have all the theological terms, but I certainly had the sense of the experience, the understanding of the moment. I had an idea that He would care for me in my failures – no matter how bad they were.

Driving with friends may have a tenuous relationship with the resurrection. However, both experiences are really about life, hope and the possibility that it can be "all better." There is still enough of the young man in me that believes that truth. I need that resurrection optimism in a world where everything didn't work out like I thought it would.

"All say, 'How hard it is that we have to die' – a strange complaint to come from the mouths of people who have had to live."

Mark Twain

Life and Death

I have spent the past week in Granada, Spain, with around 2,000 people gathered to discuss the realities of mobilizing, training and caring for Latin missionaries throughout the world.

I met with a number of leaders and talked through strategy, healthy partnerships and training. However, that is not what is going to remain in my memory from this time.

On Thursday, I was walking from my hotel to the conference center. Crossing a rather picturesque pedestrian bridge, I happened to look into the small river flowing below just as the lady walking next to me began to scream. Looking again at the scene below me I realized that I was gazing at the body of a naked man... a very dead, naked man.

While the Spanish lady next to me began

to yell into her cell phone (Note to self: scream-ing rarely helps the police identify the location of a possible crime), I took in several details very quickly. The man seemed to be in his late 30's. His tan lines indicated that he had spent a great deal of time out of doors. The strangest thing about him was that he looked so normal. He could have been one of my friends.

I won't bore you with the details of the next few minutes. After all the excitement was over and I had resumed my now rather somber walk to the meetings, I kept wondering how that man had begun his day. I wondered if he had any idea that this was going to be his last day on earth. And, as I walked to a conference of missions people, I couldn't help wondering if he had ever heard about the Jesus we claimed we were so interested in sharing with the world.

One of the things I had been thinking about even before seeing this poor fellow's "earthly tent with no one home" was how little I had heard about Jesus Christ this week. Lots of strategy, lots of dreams and lots of new tools, but not much Jesus.

I love being a missionary. It is how Susan and I have chosen to invest most of our adult lives. Still, none of this has any value if we forget what it is all about. Jesus. It is that simple. It is not brain science or rocket theory. It is a simple message for simple people.

I still wonder if anyone had ever shared that simple message with my friend from the river.

"Death is more universal than life; everyone dies but not everyone lives."

A. Sachs

More Dead Men

I know. I should leave the subject of death and mortal destruction. However, I really need to tell one more "dead man" story from Granada, Spain. If I don't do it now, I am afraid Su won't give me another chance.

This time the dead guy has a name, and we know something about his story.

Many of you have seen the movie *Braveheart*. Among some of the leaders I work with, this movie has taken on an almost "canonical" position in their understanding of leadership and commitment. Still, a movie should not be given a poor review simply because we are forced to watch out-of-context clips ad nauseam at training seminars. However, if one more person begins a seminar screaming, "Freedom!" in an imitation of Mel Gibson, I may be forced to start my own rebellion.

WOODY AND SUSAN ROLAND

If you have seen the movie, you will remember the Scottish noble named Robert the Bruce who betrayed William Wallace. According to Erwin Raphael McManus, author of *The Barbarian Way*, Robert the Bruce later rose up to lead Scotland to freedom after Wallace's execution.

Shortly before his death in 1329, Robert the Bruce requested that his heart be removed from his body and taken on a crusade by some worthy knight. James Douglas was at his bedside and took on the responsibility for his close friend. The heart was embalmed and placed in a small container that Douglas wore around his neck in every battle in which he fought. He literally carried the heart of his king pressed close to his chest.

In the early spring of 1330, Douglas sailed from Scotland to Granada, Spain, in an attempt to free that city from the Moors. (Granada would not fall until 1492.)

In his final battle, James Douglas found himself surrounded. His failure was almost certain. With the Moors closing in, Douglas reached for the heart hanging around his neck, flung it into the enemy's midst, and cried out, "Fight for the heart of your king!" One historian quotes James Douglas as saying, "Forward, brave heart, as ever thou were wont to do, and Douglas will follow his king's heart or die!"

I tried to read that passage to Susan while we were in a hospital waiting room this week, and I began to cry. In fact, as I write it out to you I am holding back the tears. I have to; it is Susan's computer and she would get upset if I ruined the keyboard.

I so want to follow my own King's heart wherever it leads! I can only hope that I am not found wanting in the key moments in life and ministry that require that kind of bravery – and incredibly eloquent words.

"Irony is a disciplinarian feared only by those who do not know it, but cherished by those who do"

Soren Kierkegaard

Isn't It Ironic?

Ironic: Both coincidental and contradictory in a humorous or poignant and extremely improbable way.

Some people say that we live in the age of irony, a time when we pay more attention to the ironic than the truthful. I hope not.

In 1996, Alanis Morissette recorded her hit song, "Ironic." If you remember the words, it is amazing how little authentic irony appeared in the piece. There is nothing ironic about rain on your wedding day. That probably should be defined as simple, bad luck. Now, if you were marrying a weatherman and he set the date and it rained on your wedding day, that would be ironic – in a sick, humorous kind of way.

I always appreciate my conversations with Susan after our devotions together. There is nothing ironic about that statement. However, we began talking about irony in the Bible one morning this week. There is more of it than you might think.

It seems ironic to me that Psalm 80 is set to a sweet-sounding tune like "Lilies of the Covenant" and still includes the lines: "O Lord God Almighty, how long will your anger smolder against the prayers of your people? You have fed them with the bread of tears; you have made them drink tears by the bowlful" (Psalm 80:4,5). If writing a psalm with that content, I would have been tempted to also write a melody entitled, "The Iron Hand of God."

It seems ironic to me that in the moment Paul's spiritual eyes were opened, his physical ones were closed (Acts 9:8). Of course, that happens to more of us than we might at first realize. Some of us were very aware of current philosophies and political movements until we met Jesus. Afterwards, we became comparably blind to those things as we followed after our Master. Some people kept a record of every hurt or slight they ever experienced before they came to know Jesus. Afterward, they couldn't have been bothered with those small things. Maybe we all should become a little blind when our eyes are opened by Him.

It seems to be the epitome of irony that where Jesus was crucified there was also a garden (John 19:41). How do you combine something so terrible with something so beautiful? The Bible does it well.

GOD SAVE THE EGGS!

Amy Carmichael, writing about God's presence during illness and pain, stated, "The Bible is amazing. Continually things that differ as much as things can, are bound together by golden chains." I like that word picture. The least become the greatest. The last become first. The mourners are filled with joy. That which seems at first to be so ironic becomes a simple statement of truth.

"One man with courage makes a majority."
Andrew Jackson

How to Kill a Lion on a Snowy Day

I have a confession to make.

Even though many people view me as an aging "rock 'n roller," I enjoy listening to sermons on my iPod. I also enjoy listening to old time radio programs, but that is irrelevant to this essay. Even in Central America, all of these can be downloaded from the Internet.

Recently, Susan and I enjoyed hearing a message given by Ray Stedman sometime in the mid-seventies. He spoke from 1 Chronicles 11:22 about "How to Kill a Lion on a Snowy Day."

Now, I must admit that, until this point in my Christian life, I have not paid too much attention to 1 Chronicles 11:22. However, I believe that it will stay with me for the rest of this long, strange trip I have here on the planet Earth. It reads, "Benaiah son of Jehoiada was a valiant fighter from Kabzeel, who performed great exploits. He struck down two of Moab's best men. He also went down into a pit on a snowy day and killed a lion." (NIV)

We are not told how he did it, but Benaiah faced the worst enemy that he could imagine in one of the worst places while under the most difficult circumstances possible. A lion is capable of killing a man simply by hitting him with his front paw. It is not necessary for him to use the whole gruesome teeth thing. If I were forced to fight a lion, I wouldn't want to do it in a pit. It would remove the illusion of mobility. If I had to fight the lion in a pit, I certainly wouldn't want to do it on a snowy day. I may live in the tropics, but I seem to remember snow doesn't provide the best footing possible.

The most ferocious enemy, in the worst place, under the most difficult conditions. Maybe you have felt like you have been in that situation before.

It is frustrating that we are not told how Benaiah did it. There is no detailed description of the feat. The Bible leaves it to our imagination. However, there are a few clues to be discovered in the passage.

Whenever Benaiah is mentioned in Scripture, it is in the context of being his father's son. He never gets to be plain, old Benaiah. He is always the son of Jehoiada.

Although I am not an expert in Hebrew, I understand that Jehoiada means, "God sees."

GOD SAVE THE EGGS!

Nothing escapes God's attention. He doesn't miss a detail. He understands what we are going through.

Benaiah means, "God builds." It is His work. He is the one that has to do it – even if "it" means facing our worst enemy. God knows what we are going through and He is the one that will carry us through. There is no doubt about it.

For the past two years Susan and I have been slogging through the ordeal of building a house in Costa Rica. To say the least, it has been a challenge. At times we didn't know if we would make it.

Yesterday, we moved in.

God saw what was happening and God built. I have no doubt about that. Though we are thankful that we have moved into our new home, our ordeal is far from being over. Yesterday, when the engineer finally showed up with the cable for our electrical installation, I fired him. Tomorrow we start from scratch. May our Father allow us to use the house for His honor and glory for as long as He gives us stewardship over it. And, may He give us steady footing in this "snowy ground."

> "When in doubt, mumble; when in trouble, delegate; when in charge, ponder."
>
> *James H. Boren*

Mumble, Mumble

I've been dealing with ongoing pain in my right foot. While in the USA, I saw a podiatrist who fitted me with a temporary insole that helps relieve the pain. Once back in Costa Rica, in my desire to have a more lasting version of that insole, I checked out the only nearby store that sells custom-fit orthotics.

I made a phone call to ask about the store hours. The woman who answered my call brought back fond memories of a cartoon I enjoyed as a child. The bear featured in that Saturday morning program always mumbled unintelligibly.

But the last two words of each line were easy to understand. You had to catch his meaning by combining the context with the hint of the final two words of his statement. (Since I have spent most of my adult life trying to understand a second language, maybe my fascination with that old bear was a foreshadowing of my future!) In answer to my question about their hours, the woman had replied something like, "Mumble, mumble, mumble, Saturday, mumble, mumble, mumble, noon."

I looked at my watch and hurried through my errands so that I could arrive well before noon. The "Orthopedic Center" eerily reminded me of the allergist's office Kari and I had visited previously.

It looked like it might spontaneously combust. Posters hung on the yellowed walls, announcing cultural events from the last century and warning of problems associated with flat feet. The "mumbly bear" woman looked on disinterestedly as I took the orthopedic insole out of my shoe to show her what the podiatrist in the US had given me. I asked if they could make something similar. Another woman who looked and sounded like her sister - both in desperate need of speech pathology – stepped out from the back room. I sensed she was curious about a real live customer showing up.

I explained to the sisters how my temporary insole has cushions on both edges in order to keep pressure off the center of the ball of my foot – the location of the inflamed nerve causing me pain. They became animated as they pulled out a special orthotic they were convinced would help. "Mumble, mumble need mumble solid bar mumble ball of your foot!"

"No, I want to keep pressure off that area of my foot."

"No! Mumble, mumble, mumble solid bar mumble, mumble, ball of your foot. Mumble, mumble try it!"

They were both so enthusiastic, I hated to let them down. I put in their special insole and stepped on it.

"OUCH! That hurts!"

Undeterred by my cry, they pulled out another insole. This one had a solid, built-up cushion right in the center. Exactly the opposite of what I was looking for. They were insistent. Being the compliant person I am, I tried it. I tried not to howl in pain.

"This one hurts even more!"

Puzzled by their unsuccessful attempts, they pulled out an empty appointment book, hoping to fill an appointment slot for the orthopedist who comes to their office twice a week. Looking around the dingy office, I wondered what type of doctor would dare venture through the door!

They badgered me with possible appointment dates as I tried to get them to refocus on what I needed – another insole like my first one. My compliant self was slowly learning self-assertion. I refused any and all offers of appointments.

Changing tacks, they started in on my flat feet. "You really need an insole to correct that!"

I've never had a problem related to my flat

feet. I didn't even want to go there. I finally thought I had them convinced to go with my initial plan, but they mumbled something which I interpreted to mean, "The man who makes the insoles is at the bank. He'll be right back."

I opted to wait, since I knew of no other options for getting a new insole. By now, they had locked their doors for lunch, but I continued to sit. Fifteen minutes later the smoke and dirt and disorder were getting to me. I announced, "I must leave. Please open the door for me."

"Oh, no! Don't leave! We see him outside the door right now!"

As I observed the figure outside, chatting with a guard, I considered my options. He would have been about my height except for his slump. A cigarette hung dangling from his lip with an accumulation of an inch of ash. His hair was either intentionally greased or hadn't been washed in ages. As they let him in, I realized he spoke much as the women, only there were fewer intelligible words among the mumbles. I actually had to resort to asking the women for interpretation!

I must say I am glad that God doesn't mumble. Even when He speaks quietly, He speaks in an understandable fashion. When Elijah heard the "soft whisper of a voice" (1 Kings 19:12) he knew it was God, and he understood what God said.

I must abbreviate the story – the smoking

craftsman first insisted on keeping my insole for a pattern. He also insisted I have identical orthotics for both feet. Finally we settled on a plan for him to diagram my current insole – and do one only for my affected right foot.

On Tuesday I picked up the insole he made. It is beautifully crafted, to be honest. It hurts like crazy and is totally useless, but, I have to confess: it's beautifully made.

"Never invest in any idea you can't illustrate with a crayon."

Peter Lynch

Invest Early

"Invest early, invest often and enjoy the miracle of compound interest." This financial strategy has been stated many times by experts trying to help people with their personal finances.

Unfortunately, I have not been blessed with excellent business skills. I seems like I have always bought late, not enough and just when the smart money was getting out. However, that doesn't mean I have been bad with my investments.

Let me explain.

When we arrived in La Paz, Bolivia, one of the young men in whom I first invested my time was David Quiroga. A young social studies teacher looking for answers, David trusted in Jesus as his Savior at a Luis Palau campaign. Through our work with those meetings, we came into contact with David a few days after he made this decision.

David began to come to our house regularly. He played table games with us. He discussed politics with us. We studied the Bible together. David began to grow in his faith and later became one of my students at the seminary.

Since then, David has planted several churches. His most recent church plant in Bolivia is located in one of the poorer barrios in the city of Cochabamba. I like to think of some of those people with whom David shares, people I have never met, beginning to walk with the Lord. Talk about compound interest!

David is not the only one in whom we invested early.

Dino was a young rebel. He attended our church in La Paz for over six months before he made a decision. He has now spent the past twenty years in ministry in Paraguay. Another man, Nelson, caused me no end of trouble as a young man. Since his rough beginning, he has planted three churches in the greater Buenos Aires area. Rene used to beat the woman with whom he lived. Today, he is a national leader in a well-known ministry.

Investing early makes sense.

I am thankful for the men who invested in me. My relationship with my father had a few serious bumps, all caused by my rather interesting personality. I am extremely thankful for his patience, love and tenacity in reaching out to me. I believe he thinks his investment was worthwhile. However, considering how much he had to put in, it would be understandable if he felt there should have been a higher pay-out.

My father-in-law opened my mind through wide-ranging discussions. There is no doubt that some of who I am today is the result of his investment in that young hippie who showed up on his doorstep asking for his daughter.

Mel Connell was the pastor of the first church I attended after becoming a Christian. I have to give Mel all the credit in the world. Even though I had caused him problems earlier on in his ministry, he didn't think twice about investing in me. Try to imagine a holiness preacher with thick-rimmed glasses walking around with a young man with hair down to his shoulders.

We were probably the original odd couple.

When I moved to Texas, God brought me into contact with John Faulkner. At the time, John was president of a foundation and vice-president of a college. To me he was a man with a deep knowledge of Scripture who allowed me to ask questions.

I am afraid my questions have caused a lot of other people to shake their heads.

Kevin Dyer founded International Teams. Kevin invested in me by opening doors at key points in my life. He also gave me one of my life mottos: "Make a decision and make it right." I have tried Kevin, I really have.

WOODY AND SUSAN ROLAND

Sometimes I think we miss what Jesus was about. If you ask a Christian why Jesus came to earth, most of them will respond, "To die for our sins." That is true, but there is more that we probably need to see. Admittedly, the will of God was that Jesus would come and die. Unfortunately for us, it is also God's will for us. We need to die to ourselves. That often seems like a long, painful process to me. The work of Jesus was something different. In John 17:4, Jesus said, "I have shown your glory on earth; I have finished the work you gave me to do."

What was that work? The simple answer is: investing in making disciples of others. After three or three and a half years of public ministry, Jesus could honestly say to his heavenly Father, "I have done everything that I could by investing in these fellows. I am going to have to trust You to work out Your will through them as they continue on."

Twelve men. No, it was really only eleven! Still, the "compound interest" seems to have paid off. Christianity managed to take off based on the investment Jesus made.

We probably all wish that we had invested early and more regularly, but it is never too late. Today might be a good day for us to look around and think about who we should invest in. Who knows? Maybe something could actually come from spending time with that odd-looking kid with the earring and tattoo in the back of your church.

You never know where he might end up.

"Any simple problem can be made unsolvable if enough meetings are held to discuss it."

Unknown

Meeting Hater

I do not like meetings. It has been my thought for some time that Christianity would have been a wonderful religion if we hadn't included so many meetings in the whole experience. People who work closely with me know that if they want me to attend a meeting, I first need to know the reason we are having the meeting; the possible solutions we should consider; and our most probable outcome. One of my co-workers has pointed out that, given my parameters, there is little reason left for meeting with me.

I agree.

Of course, there are all types of meetings. While I do not enjoy business meetings, I do genuinely appreciate meeting with friends.

Unfortunately, because of our ministry lifestyle, I often have to meet my close friends "on the run." There is rarely enough time to relax and enjoy each other as I would like.

I have one friend who makes it a point to meet me in the Minneapolis airport when I fly through. He claims he is concerned that I will not know where I am if I don't see his face. He is probably right. He also usually lends me a coat.

I once met a pastor in a pub in downtown London. I found it interesting that the pub was decorated with stained glass windows. I found it even more interesting that one of the stained glass windows commemorated the life of C.T. Studd, the great missionary hero. This could only happen in England. This past weekend, after trips to Israel and South Carolina (for meetings!), we had the privilege of seeing a few of our friends in East Texas.

Jack Faulkner has been a friend of mine since we both knew better. He has the habit of having his birthday each year on March 17th. This year his wife, Karen, allowed us to surprise him for the occasion. It was worth the effort and expense to see him fall back in his chair with surprise – and we have the photo to prove it. We took advantage of being in the area to catch up with our friends, Ed and Lu Ann. We had to find a restaurant to meet them about half way between where they lived and where we were staying. We knew we couldn't go wrong with a barbecue place named "Vernon´s."

It didn't let us down.

GOD SAVE THE EGGS!

After supper, Susan declared her need (you may define this as "obsession") for some ice cream. Now, when you are in East Texas and you are looking for ice cream, the only thing that should come to your mind is "Blue Bell." It really is some of the finest ice cream in the world. Unfortunately, we couldn't find a restaurant in Conroe, Texas, that served it.

Something as small as that was not going to keep my wife away from her hankering.

Susan, Ed, Lu Ann and I found ourselves eating pints of ice cream between aisles 10 and 11 at the local Kroger's grocery store. I can verify the table we used is a real bargain at $99.00 (four chairs included). If you are ever through there, you might want to consider buying them. I am sure the manager who gave us permission to sit there would appreciate it.

I believe something like this could only happen in Texas. People in Texas understand the need for good ice cream and for meeting with friends. I was impressed during my visit to Jerusalem that one day our Lord will return to meet us just like he left this earth.

1 Thessalonians 4:17 says, "…then those of us who are still living will be caught up along with them on clouds in the air to meet the Lord, and so we shall be with the Lord forever." Now, *that* will be a meeting I do not want to miss. It probably beats all the ice cream in Texas – even the Blue Bell consumed between aisles 10 and 11.

"May you live every day of your life"
Jonathan Swift

Getting Renewed at the Department of Motor Vehicles

One bright June day I spent the morning in the offices of the Costa Rican equivalent of the Department of Motor Vehicles. Once again, it was time to renew my driver's license.

Well, that is not completely true. It was time to renew my license in March. June was "way past time" according to the gentleman at the first desk I approached. So, he politely but firmly added a 5,000 colon fine to my driver's license fee. I did not argue the legal technicalities.

Since the process to renew my license can require several hours of waiting in four separate lines, it provides a unique opportunity to reflect on life and what I am doing with my own. The fact that Susan and I were celebrating 31 years of marriage this particular day probably added to my reflective nature.

Marriage has a way of encouraging personal reflection, doesn't it guys?

Not long ago, someone asked me why I had "given up my life" to be a missionary. I found that to be an interesting question, one that deserved some contemplation. At least, it seemed like it deserved thought while waiting to have my photo taken for my new license.

I think what was really behind this person's question is the growing lack of understanding in society, as a whole, of people giving their lives for any purpose that does not involve personal gain. How are you going to benefit? What is the bottom line? These types of questions do not combine well with the missionary lifestyle.

It seems like anyone willing to give their life for a cause is suspect. He or she must be a radical, a religious fanatic or worse. The idea that some causes are worth our lives seems to belong to a simpler, far-off time. Either that, or the idea of giving your life for a cause has become the sole prerogative of Muslim radicals.

* * *

Thinking of simpler times took me back to the classic story of Mucius, a Roman patriot.

Unfortunately, Mucius is almost forgotten today. It could be because his name sounds too much like mucus to seriously inspire the imagination of junior high boys. Or, it could be because his type of dedication and willingness to sell his life for the cause is so out of date.

When Porsena, the Etruscan king, was laying siege to the upstart city of Rome, a Roman youth named Mucius snuck out of the city and made his way into Porsena's camp. While looking on from the sidelines, Mucius saw an important-looking person surrounded by officers and giving orders. Drawing his conclusion and dagger, Mucius ran to the gentleman and buried his weapon in the stomach of what Mucius took to be the king.

Unfortunately, for both him and the victim, Mucius had killed the king's personal secretary. As punishment, King Porsena sentenced young Mucius to be burned to death. Before the soldiers could carry out the sentence, the boy made this statement to the king: "I came to kill you and failed. You may execute me for that. I will not weep at the honor of laying down my life for my city." As he continued, he stuck his hand into the nearby flames and shouted, "Do not rejoice, but see the determination of a Roman. For after me will come another, and another, and another."

While he made this impressive statement, his hand burned in the flames. According to tradition, Mucius didn't flinch or otherwise respond to the pain.

King Porsena was absolutely stunned by this young man's virtue, dedication and manly courage. In fact, he was so impressed that he ordered the soldiers to set Mucius free.

As you can imagine, Mucius' hand was useless from that day on. Because of that, the men of Rome gave him the nickname of Scaevola, or "Lefty." It seems that Mucius bore his new name with a certain pride, and it commanded respect for years to come.

Men (and boys) like Mucius are hard to find these days. They were men who embraced the risk of the moment because although they were dispensable, their cause was not. They believed some causes were worth the ultimate sacrifice.

* * *

I finally waded through all the lines and received my new license. Once again, my photo makes me think that I may be deader than King Porsena's secretary. It was time to get back to San Isidro and see if I was still willing to pay the price.

"One always wonders about roads not taken."
Warren Christopher

Extreme Baby Shower

xtreme baby shower. Sounds like an oxymoron, doesn't it?

I suppose being 16 years old and expecting twin boys comes close to an oxymoron as well.

Yesterday I four-wheeled an hour off the main road on the other side of the valley to attend a baby shower for Nena's 16-year-old daughter. Mountain folk often marry young, as is the case of Tatiana. She was married at age 15 and now is expecting twin boys!

Those of you who know me well know that I love jeeping in the mountains and that I have plenty of experience with the remote stretch of road that winds and jolts its way to Nena's house.

Yesterday gave me reason to pause three times, get out of "Su's Zuki," and actually lay

WOODY AND SUSAN ROLAND

hands on the Sidekick and pray!

My first stop came after I opted to take a newly carved road which I thought would circumvent a dicey stretch on the old path. After lurching down the wet, slippery, red clay slope for about a quarter of a mile, I slowly came to the realization not only that the two roads were not joining up again, but also that there were no recent tire tracks on my path. I parked the car and in my dress and sandals hiked down a bit further to verify those facts. There was no option but to back up. Vision in reverse on a steep slope, trying to peer over the spare tire is difficult at best. The jeep skittered on the clay incline. After about three blocks in reverse I decided the road was just wide enough to turn around. After a ten-point turn and bumping up against a barbed wire fence, I could finally breathe a sigh of relief and use first gear, low four-wheel to return to the original "road."

I thought the rest of the drive would be "all downhill." It *was* all downhill, but not in the sense of being *easy*. The water-laden mountainsides made it necessary to creep along in first gear most of the way. I was only about a half mile from Nena's when my heart jumped. The road ahead did not look familiar. As I drew closer, I realized why.

Part of the mountainside had come down onto the narrow road! Fortunately, the tree that came down technically was not on the roadway, *but* 2 feet of soft mud and grass

152

were. Oh, my! There was no way to back up this time. I once again parked the car, got out, and prayed. My only options were to rely on Zuki and God's hand or wade through the mud and walk the final half mile, leaving Zuki right there. I carefully evaluated the situation, my pulse racing.

Gravity would pull me straight ahead on the downward slope, which was an advantage. There was no significant precipice off to the left – another advantage. The precipice that lay on the other side of the mudslide was preceded by at least 12 feet of solid road. So, with my heart in my throat, I slithered through the mud and had to only maneuver the car twice on the other side to head down what now looked like an awfully sweet piece of road.

Thank You, Lord!

It took at least fifteen minutes for my heart to calm once I got to the shower. Since I arrived early, I helped Tatiana fry chicharrones and finish preparations for the shower. It was such a privilege to be there as part of the family in that remote mountain community! Nena asked me to give the welcome and begin the shower with a prayer – an anomaly in this very Catholic area!

Several neighbors were amazed that I'd driven down that mountain stretch alone! They strongly suggested that I return by the road that leads down to Vuelta de Jorco instead of chancing the dreaded curve and landslides on the road above. Their comments about the Jorco road were not terribly encouraging. "That road was closed yesterday because the river was over it, but it's not too bad today."

OK, Lord! Protect me once again!

The road to Jorco was barely recognizable. It was obvious that the river had recently claimed portions of it as its own bed. It presented no unexpected challenges, however, until I was almost down to the town.

As I rounded one of the final curves, my heart once again skipped a few beats. This shower was proving to be a true cardiac stress test! The left twenty percent of the road was now lying twenty feet below me, literally in the river. On the remaining road I could see a channel of water measuring one and a half feet wide and a half foot deep cutting straight through the remaining road.

If I were to attempt to continue, I would have to trust that the narrow strip of dirt on my left would not decide to join the rest of the road lying somewhere far below. If I attempted to cross the channel too slowly, my tires would potentially drop the half foot down, never to budge again. At whatever speed, the whole section could give way.

With a gulp and a prayer, I charged straight across the channel, keeping my left tire on the one piece of intact land. Zuki managed to drop both sets of wheels quickly in and out of the channel while God's hand held up the muddy rut.

GOD SAVE THE EGGS!

Usually baby showers are associated with women chatting, drinking tea, playing games and oohing and ahhing over baby clothes. This one would have made an exciting episode on reality TV. But, I guess that's what our Christian walk should be all about – living by faith and not by sight.

"It is an illusion that youth is happy, an illusion of those who have lost it."

W. Somerset Maugham

Looking Forward, Looking Back

In my never-ending quest to provide helpful and useful information that can improve the quality of the lives of our supporters, I would like to share a few lessons learned from the waiting room at the hospital where Susan had her surgery a little while ago.

1. Avoid prolonged sitting in the chairs provided in Latin America hospitals. While the paralysis is not permanent, it is uncomfortable. Even sadists must have useful employment. We now know they design hospital furniture in Costa Rica.

2. Always have companions with whom you can wait. Seriously. It was a joy to have Kari with me on Friday, even though she now talks like a secondary school teacher. Considering how well I

got on with my own junior high and senior high teachers (or, didn't!), I feel like I
have come a long way.

3. No matter how long you wait, the doctor will show up when you have
stepped out for a few minutes. Possible
solutions: Eat no food, drink no liquids
and have yourself catheterized before
your spouse begins the surgery. I will
admit this is uncomfortable, but at the
very least you will be able to talk to the
surgeon or attending physician.

4. Remember, in Latin America, births and
surgeries often take place in the same
facility and on the same floor. This
means there are two types of people
waiting: (mostly) young family members
waiting for the new baby and (mostly)
older folks having incredibly nasty things
done to loved ones. This is kind of like
putting committed Democrats and Re-
publicans in the same coffee shop – at
election time.

I was reminded of something that I read
this week. In Ezra 3:12 it says, "But many of the
older priests and Levites and family heads,
who had seen the former temple, wept aloud
when they saw the foundation of this temple
being laid, while many others shouted for joy."
On the day the new foundations of the ruined
temple were laid in Jerusalem after seventy
years in exile, the reactions of the generations

were markedly different. The young people were happy, even excited. The old folks were dismayed. Their cheeks wore no smiles, but were bathed in tears. They remembered the glory of the former temple.

Young people look forward; old folks look back. Youth embraces the future, where most of its life lies; old age thinks about the past, where most of its life has gone.

One of the great truths of Christianity is that we need both the young and the "more mature." Enthusiasm without experience can lead to new efforts crashing in flames. Experience without enthusiasm can often mean the new efforts never take off.

Having younger people waiting with Kari and me was a gentle reminder of the joys of life, even while Susan experienced some of the frustrations of other realities.

"If there were no God, there would be no atheists."

G. K. Chesterton

Bathroom Reading

I have attempted to find a tasteful way to state something about myself. However, I can't. So, I am simply going to say it: I read in the bathroom.

I believe this habit (which many of you will find disgusting and a sign of my admittedly coarse manners) traces itself back to my parents' subscription to *Reader's Digest*. A great part of my formal education came from that magazine, and I am deeply indebted to its editors.

Recently I finished a book that I began two years ago. The length of time required to complete the book could be related to several factors – all of which I refuse to go into in this public format. However, it is sufficient to say that the book has been a good companion.

WOODY AND SUSAN ROLAND

Richard Osborne's *Philosophy for Beginners* started out well, but ended in a rather confused state. This probably has something to do with the content itself. Philosophy back in the day of Socrates, Plato and Heraclitus ("You cannot step into the same river twice") may have been mistaken, but it was understandable. By the time I got to Roland Barthes ("All reality is myth, a form of narrative"), Jacques Derrida and Jean-Paul Sartre, philosophy became a bit dense for my limited capabilities.

Still, even for me, it has been easy to understand that one of the biggest mega-trends of secular philosophy of the last two centuries has been the idea that God is no longer the source of truth. During my travels last year, I was amazed at how many popular books about atheism were for sale in airports throughout the world. Through best-sellers by Richard Dawkins and Christopher Hitchens, the world was informed that God hasn't made Himself known because, according to them, there is no one there to be made known.

Even though these popular books are currently jumping off the airport bookstands, the "Golden Age of Atheism" really took place over 200 years ago with the French Revolution. Around that time, Voltaire suggested the attractiveness of atheism was in direct relation to the corruption of the major Christian institutions. I wonder if he wasn't right. Popular interest in atheism today probably has more to do with a general failure by Christians to live as real disciples than any innate desire by people to become "frothing-at-the-mouth-atheists."

Even though Marx is generally thought of in the political and economic realm, he was primarily a philosopher. Marx believed that ideas and values are determined by the material realities of life. He also believed that religion eases pain by creating a fantasy world where people can hide from their sorrows.

I don't know about you, but I do not believe Christianity is a place where I can lose myself in my fantasies and experience no difficulties. In fact, when I think about it, a lot of the pain I have experienced in life is a direct result of being a Christian. I have been forced to face difficult and hard issues in my own life through my walk with Jesus. If I hadn't been a Christian, I would have experienced other problems. However, I cannot agree with Marx (even if he did have a great hair style) that Christianity is a free pass from reality.

Freud was a philosopher disguised as a psychiatrist. For him, religion was an illusion that drew its strength from our instinctual desires. Also, as an atheist, he believed that religion was dangerous. While he was alive, many people accepted Freud's criticisms of religion because they seemed scientific. My guess is that acceptance of Freud's thoughts had more to do with people wanting to escape the reality of their own sinfulness than their sudden embrace of science as their favorite subject in school.

WOODY AND SUSAN ROLAND

Now, having said all this, I have to confront a painful reality about myself... once again.

It seems to me that in some deep, dark part of my life, I wish the atheists were right. I would feel more shame about this confession except that I believe the same is true for all of us.

Every time I decide to follow my own will rather than submit to God's, I have shown myself to be a practical atheist. Every time I choose not to trust Him with my needs, I prove the weakness of my faith. In the moment I hide in my room with my unconfessed sin, like Adam in the garden, and hope that He will not come calling my name, I am no different from non-believers who have come before me.

The fact is, it would be easy for me to look down my rather prominent nose at authors like Dawkins and Hitchens except for the fact that they are open about the disbelief that I often try to disguise in my sin.

Fortunately, the reality of God's existence has nothing to do with my beliefs, non-belief or propensity to sin. He exists in His own right. He always has and He always will.

In His interactions with His own creation, God has made a career out of dealing with practical "non-believers" like me.

Back in a day when His people had mixed true belief about God with other religions and philosophies, He told the prophet Amos, "If they dig deep into the earth or climb to the sky, I'll reach out and get them. If they escape to the peaks of Mount Carmel, I'll search and find them. And if they hide from me at the bottom of the ocean, I'll command a sea monster to bite them... When the LORD God All-Powerful touches the earth, it melts, and its people mourn." (Amos 9)

It seems to me that if my last name is Dawkins or Hitchens or even Roland, it might be worthwhile to look over my shoulder from time to time to see what is going to bite me in the seat of my pants. There is no place to hide from a God who really exists, no matter what we might have read or thought in our more private moments.

"Water, air, and cleanness are the chief articles in my pharmacy."

Napoleon Bonaparte

H_2O

People in Latin America do not need as much personal space as most of you in the United States. Men in Minnesota greet each other face on, and then turn to create a 135 degree angle from the front of each other's bodies. This is often the key moment when corn prices (the most intimate topic good friends share about) are discussed. Texans tend to come in a bit closer for the actual handshake, but separate for the conversation. I suppose this makes it easier to draw a concealed weapon if there is any untoward disagreement.

Men in most of Latin America have been known to stand so close to each other during conversations they actually touch.

This may be why I do not meet many Minnesotans in Costa Rica.

WOODY AND SUSAN ROLAND

Of course, we do not raise much corn, either. Conversation topics would be severely limited.

Toward the end of this week, I have noticed that people are standing a bit off from me. It is rather like they are finally developing a sense of awareness to my birth culture. I have to admit it seems a bit odd. In fact, when they can, they are also beginning to stand upwind from me.

I should explain that during the last week, we have not had much water. Truth be told, I have not had a shower since Monday. I am not sure, but this could be why my Latin friends are developing cultural sensitivity at this late point in our relationship. Bio-diversity sounds good on the Discovery Channel but tends to smell a bit raw up close and in your personal space.

I should also explain that Costa Rica is at the end of its dry season, and apparently we have used up all our water.

Because our water supplies are low, we are also low on electricity. The entire central valley is experiencing rolling blackouts. The government says these should only last for three hours at a time. However, we have been through several six and seven hour periods without power. The government also says the blackouts should not impact hospitals, schools or tourism. Still, the hospitals are turning away new patients; schools are in the dark; and, tourists are bumping and sniffing their way through the darkness like anyone else.

The national concern about personal hygiene aside, I think many people are taking this with good grace. We may not smell too good, but we are all in this together.

Our current situation became a bit surreal when Susan and I drove by a mall with electricity and decided to take a few moments to observe each other in the light. As we walked hand in hand (with a healthy distance separating us), we both began to notice the background music. Without really thinking about it, we began to sing with the ersatz piano music. "Wonderful grace of Jesus, greater than all my sin..." By the time we reached the "rolling sea" in the chorus, we had both begun to wonder who was choosing the music for the mall.

Of course, at that very moment all the lights went out.

Fortunately, we were near the exit, could smell the others around us, and made it to our car without too many difficulties. Besides that, we went off with the knowledge that His grace would be with us – wherever and to whatever depth of ocean or however shallow the reserves.

"Sudden resolutions, like the sudden rise of mercury in a barometer, indicate little else than the variability of the weather."

David Hare

Resolved!

The Puritans were not big on celebrating the New Year. As a matter of fact, they were downright against it. Instead of celebrations, they encouraged young men to think soberly about the coming year and resolve how to live holier lives in it.

Apparently this early, U.S. tradition has been somewhat diluted in recent centuries.

Jonathan Edwards wrote 70 resolutions when he was 19 or 20 by which he determined to live his life. One of those resolved to "never speak anything ridiculous... or (a) matter of laughter on the Lord's Day."

This might explain "Sinners in the Hands of an Angry God."

Although it was not in his list of 70 resolutions, Edwards' commitment to study the Scriptures for 13 hours each day certainly cut him off from the life of his church. Of course, on the up side, at least his congregation did not have to worry about their pastor getting involved in illicit relationships. From the news that I have received from around Christendom in the last six months, perhaps it would be good for many pastoral workers to resolve to spend more time in the Word and less doing embarrassing things.

We have had the privilege of knowing David and Rennie Garda for a number of years. The Gardas helped found and currently direct Cadre Ministries. In a brief explanation of why he hadn't been sending out so many emails of late, David wrote, "I've been wrestling (with) applying what I've learned from studying the getaways of Jesus. I don't know anyone who filled his days more intentionally with ministry than my hero Jesus. At the same time he never let his priorities get turned upside down by anyone else. He took responsibility for his mentoring, his pace and his soul. I want to live that way, too!"

A brief look at how Jesus took time away from ministry shows that He got away 21 times in 3 ½ years of public ministry. He spent about half of His getaways alone and the rest with His ministry team. He got away with four main purposes: to pray; to rest; to equip others; and to align with His father's will.

I have never been big on making New Year's resolutions. However, if I was going to make a resolution for this year, I think it would be to imitate Jesus in His getaways – especially those to align with His will. I want to make sure I do not become guilty of doing silly or embarrassing things in this ministry with which I have been entrusted.

"The true object of all human life is play. Earth is a task garden; heaven is a playground."

Gilbert K. Chesterton

No Excuses in Heaven

This past week I had to make a quick trip back to Minnesota for the funeral of my Aunt Helen. I have missed many funerals over the years, including my grandmother's and my grandfather's. It was a privilege to be present for this celebration.

When I was in high school, I would occasionally (okay – fairly often) miss the bus. Mrs. Binder, the long-suffering driver, waited for nothing or no one. Because of that, I had to hitchhike the 18 miles to school. Rides in rural Minnesota were not always easy to find for a long-haired young man. Many times I arrived after classes had begun. Being late in that school meant I needed a permission slip. Aunt Helen was my reliable source of written excuses.

Helen would not lie for me. I am not sure

she *could* lie. She simply wrote, "Woody missed the bus and is late. Please let him in. Helen." That was all it took. They never turned me down.

In July, Susan and I had the privilege of visiting with Helen in the hospice care facility where she spent her final weeks. Although the tumor or treatment had already taken her vision, she was very alert. I entered the room, reached for her hand and identified myself. The first thing she said was, "Oh, Woody! Do I need to write you an excuse, again?"

It was hard to be at Helen's funeral... and very good. I am told that 500 people came to the visitation. The actual service was attended by over 300. This included at least five people that were in my small, graduating class. I wonder if she wrote excuses for them, as well.

In our years of living in Latin America, I have been asked to perform a number of funerals.

The first funeral I ever did in La Paz, Bolivia, went without a hitch. Well, at least until I said the final prayer at the cemetery. After I said "Amen" nothing happened. Everyone continued to look at me. So, as a way of giving people permission to leave, I informed the crowd the service had ended. Still, nothing happened.

Finally, one of the young men assisting me said, "Don Woody, the pastor always closes the casket." I looked down at the wood screws in the top of the cheap, wood coffin. "Okay. Who has the screwdriver?" "Woody, the pastor always brings the screwdriver!"

It took a long time to get all those screws tightened using a five peso coin.

Once in Bolivia, I preached a funeral for a lady who wanted to be buried in her drive-way. I am not making this up! The family insisted those were her final wishes. However, I must admit the son-in-law seemed especially encouraged by the prospect of driving back to what was going to be his new home every day.

Once I had the terrible responsibility of informing a sister that her adult brother had died. One hopes that when a pastor shows up at the front door at 10:00 p.m. dressed in a dark suit and carrying a large, black Bible that people will prepare themselves to receive bad news. That is the theory anyway. On this occasion, the sister was so shocked by the news I gave her that she struck me in the face with her fist and split my lip.

Preaching a funeral looking like you have been in a bar brawl is not the easiest task in the world. Just before I was informed by telephone of my aunt's passing, Susan and I listened to a song that had already brought tears to my eyes. The words go:

"I want to stroll over Heaven with you some glad day
When all our troubles and heartaches are vanished away
Then we'll enjoy the beauty where all things are new

WOODY AND SUSAN ROLAND

I want to stroll over Heaven with you."

I am at a place in life where I look forward to "strolling over Heaven" with many loved ones that have gone before.

My grandfather and I were pretty close. He could be very gruff, but I believe he loved me. Several times I have imagined him meeting me upon my arrival in Heaven. In my mind I see him leaning forward slightly with his hands in his pockets, looking at me and saying, "You're late. What took you so long? You going to waste the whole day?"

Hopefully, Helen will still be able to write excuses for her nephew.

"You have to love a nation that celebrates its independence every July 4, not with a parade of guns, tanks, and soldiers... but with family picnics where kids throw Frisbees, the potato salad gets iffy, and the flies die from happiness. You may think you have overeaten, but it is patriotism."

Erma Bombeck

I Miss the Fourth of July

It is not as if it is not July 4th here in Central America. As I write this, it is probably the same date in most locations except for Australia. From experience, I know Australians live by their own calendar.

No, I miss the Fourth of July I knew when I was a younger man.

There was never any doubt in my mind where I was going to go on the holiday, or what I was going to do. My family had its customs, and we stood by them.

Every year we went to a picnic in Jobi's pasture. It had been a long time since the Jobi family actually owned this piece of ground, but the name remained. In rural communities, people do not change a name simply on the basis of real estate transactions. I have known locations identified by the name of the family who lived there before their house burned down forty years ago.

Jobi´s pasture was not particularly beautiful. However, it had ample space for cars, a snack stand, and a baseball diamond. The mighty Zumbro River bordered it. Tables were set up on saw horses and covered with food.

I still think of that food on the 4th. It doesn't matter where I am in the world. The memory of that holiday fare comes back to haunt me.

Of course one of the culinary highlights was the deviled eggs. Sometimes the Holiness people had a different name for them, but we all knew what they were.

Now, most young boys are very aware of the fact that deviled eggs were not meant to actually be eaten on the Fourth of July. We had other uses for them. Placing even the smallest firecracker in a deviled egg produced wonderful results – especially if someone happened to walk down the path on which you had placed this patriotic surprise.

Working pastures usually provide an abundant supply of another source of joy for young men. Be honest now, cow pies and firecrackers have a natural synergy.

How do I phrase this delicately? Like deviled eggs, the secret is in the recipe. The challenge comes in finding just the right cow pie for the right firecracker. A ladyfinger won't do.

GOD SAVE THE EGGS!

The smallest firecracker permitted is a Black Cat. Without a doubt, if they could be found, cherry bombs were the best.

Like I said, I miss the Fourth of July.

The first 4th of July Susan and I celebrated in Bolivia was hard. To celebrate our non-holiday, we decided to do something very special. We went out and found hotdogs to prepare and eat in our apartment. I can assure you it was no easy feat to find hotdogs in La Paz in those years.

I will never forget sitting around that small table, eating those hotdogs and listening to the Voice of America on the shortwave radio. We never felt so far from the United States.

I will also never forget the results those hot-dogs had on our stressed missionary digestive systems. Apparently the United States is not the only place where the Fourth was celebrated with explosive devices. I don't think we left our apartment for two days.

Some progressive Christians find themselves vaguely uncomfortable with displays of patri-otism. My guess is this has something to do with the exaggerated nationalism of the past. It may also be related to the fact that we love our country but realize it is not our ultimate home. We do not completely belong here or to any other earthly nation.

As for me, I believe that patriotism, at the very least, frees us from our natural egocentric behavior. A patriot should think of others in his society and not himself. If we are not capable of appreciating our own country, we will not be capable of appreciating that country to which we move. If we can't be loyal to "here," we won't learn to be loyal to "there."

Today, I am working in an office in Costa Rica. No one has any flags on display. There will be no fireworks tonight. Still, I think of the country I once knew so well and pray that it may once again be a source of blessing and light to all nations.

I also hope that boys still remember what to do with deviled eggs.

"Many will call me an adventurer - and that I am, only one of a different sort: one of those who risks his skin to prove his platitudes."

Che Guevara

Finding Che Guevara

This past week has been a busy one for random Che Guevara sightings.

Ernesto or "Che," as he is known throughout Latin America, was the Argentine, leftist guerilla who aided Fidel Castro in his revolution in Cuba in 1959. People throughout Latin America find a certain amount of inspiration in a man who lived (and died) according to his ideals. For some reason, commitment seems to be rare in politicians in our part of the world.

Perhaps the reason Che was in the news so much is that Monday marked the 40th anniversary of his death in Bolivia.

In 1966, after failed attempts at inciting revolution in Africa, Che disguised himself as a bald business man and flew into La Paz. During the next several months, he would lead a band of Cuban, Peruvian and, even, French guerillas in a failed attempt to bring the revolution to South America. He was ignored by the Bolivian Communist Party and, some say, betrayed by Fidel. Eventually, sick, wounded and with a malfunctioning rifle, he was taken prisoner.

Even though it goes against popular leftist myth, it would seem the senior CIA agent present actually tried to save Che's life. The U.S. government thought he would be more valuable as a prisoner than a martyr. Unfortunately, the next day Ernesto Guevara was executed by a drunken Army sergeant on the direct orders of the President of Bolivia.

The place where Che died has become a popular tourist site. People visit it with almost religious devotion. I have a feeling that Ernesto would have laughed at something so ironic.

Fifty-two Bolivian soldiers died in the campaign against Che and his international guerillas. I can't remember one of their names as I write. That seems unfair and sad. I imagine they had dreams, desires and passions as well.

Che was also in the news this week because the sergeant who killed him was operated on in Santa Cruz, Bolivia, last Monday. He had cataracts removed by Cuban physicians who are in Bolivia at the request and invitation of the Bolivian government. When asked, the doctors said they considered it an honor to help the elderly gentleman.

You can see it wasn't a complete surprise

that Che also came into my office yesterday morning. Well, Che wasn't actually feeling up to it, but his legacy in Latin America was certainly there.

Hector, the fellow in charge of our building construction on the Multiplication Center, sat with me to work through our weekly resolution of finances. As we went through the bills, he calmly told me that his uncle had been executed two weeks ago by leftist guerillas in Colombia. He refused to abandon his farm, so they made him kneel down and they decapitated him.

Hector told me that his mother responded by saying, "If they had been real men they would have just shot him." It is hard for most of us to imagine a world where being shot is considered a blessing.

The representative of the company that provides most of our building materials was also with us in the office. After listening to Hector, he began to cry. He finally calmed down enough to say, "During the war in Nicaragua I was on the government's side. I cannot tell you about the times we went out to hunt Sandinista guerillas just to capture them and torture them. I am embarrassed about what I have done."

It is kind of hard to have a man whose uncle has just been killed by leftists and a man who admits to having been on the other side of the equation of evil to both look at you with hope that you can help them find peace.

Fortunately, I do not have to.

Scripture speaks of peace in three different ways. In Romans 5:1, we find the concept of peace with God, a relationship which men can enter into by faith. The peace of God is promised to believers in Phil. 4:7. If we are willing to give Him our cares and anxieties, we can be sure He will give us His peace. Finally, in Matthew 10:34, we are told that "peace with God" and "the peace of God" will not bring immediate peace on earth. Instead, conflicts between men will continue.

Che never found personal or political peace. He died as a result of the violence he encouraged. My prayer is that my two friends will find real peace in some of the tragedies they have experienced in this troubled world.

"The rate at which a person can mature is directly proportional to the embarrassment he can tolerate."

Douglas Engelbart

Emancipated Embryos

Recently I read an article written by Gordon MacDonald that Woody sent to me. Some of you may recall that MacDonald is familiar with "muffing up." Unlike other fallen Christian leaders, MacDonald humbly repented of his sin, and God has seen fit to continue to use him, just as he used a king named David who muffed up centuries ago. MacDonald is now editor at large of Leadership magazine and chair of World Relief.

MacDonald quotes Martin Thornton, "A walloping great congregation is fine and fun, but what most communities really need is a couple of saints. The tragedy is that they may well be there in embryo, waiting to be discovered, waiting for sound training, waiting to be emancipated from the cult of the mediocre."

WOODY AND SUSAN ROLAND

Joel Osteen has made it big. Let me promise you, he has a walloping great congregation. In Houston, at what used to be the Rockets' stadium, Lakewood Church hosts three services with an average attendance of 16,000 per service. On Larry King Live, Joel was introduced as a "mega-pastor." Woody jokingly told me, "Hey! I want to be a mega-super-hyper-maxi-pastor!" Osteen's main goal is to make people feel really good about themselves and believe that God has better things for them – both in this life and the life to come.

MacDonald writes about how we as a church are not too bad at bringing people to Christ and doing basic discipleship. It is possible to have programs (and the modern church loves programs!) that bring people to Christ and take them through booklets that teach them the basics of the faith. But programs rarely produce true mature Christians.

We are good at producing "churchy Christians," but listen to how MacDonald describes the holy, Christ-like man or woman of God: "I have in mind those who walk through all the corridors of the larger life – the market-place, the home and community, the playing fields – and do it in such a way that, sooner or later, it is concluded that Jesus' fingerprints are all over them."

These are people who - just by the way they live - leave behind them a trail that makes people ready to hear about Jesus. It's hard to define a mature Christian, but you are likely to know one when you see one. The marks of maturity include a spiritual devotional life that is self-sustaining, wisdom in human relationships, humble service, and comfort in the everyday life in the real world where faith is lived out among unbelievers.

How many people do you know that are like that? Have we forgotten how to raise saints? What are we doing wrong? Reading the wrong books? Doing the wrong studies? Too much application in church of the world's principles of success?

Mature Christians are formed in many ways, but one important key is through mentoring. When I was a young wife and mother and missionary in Bolivia, I realized that I sorely needed a godly woman to mentor me. During one furlough I decided to approach several mature women who were experienced both in ministry and in being godly wives and mothers. I was disillusioned when, one after the other, they refused to share their lives and wisdom with me. One of them told me bluntly, "I have nothing to teach you." I almost got down on my knees to beg her, "Can't you teach me some of what you know about following Christ and serving others? You host many people in your home. Can you give me tips on having a healthy balance between hosting guests and caring for family? Can you at least give me some recipes that are easy to fix for big groups?"

"No."

The answer was final. My heart was broken.

WOODY AND SUSAN ROLAND

I could only go to God and say, "You have to help me! I want to do this right and well. Help me, please!"

Mentoring might involve sharing a helpful book with someone, but it goes way beyond sharing recipes and reading books. As we read that book, we talk of life and we pray about ways that God needs to change us and how to go about that. Mentoring takes place on the streets of life – learning how to live as a Christian in the nitty-gritty of life. "Mature Christians are made one by one through the influence of other Christians already mature," says MacDonald.

I've been writing a small devotional book for my daughters. Two weeks of *Su's Daily Devos* focus on the reality of suffering in our lives. Mature Christians grow through suffering. A sense of inadequacy is the stepping stone to dependency on God. Wrestling with questions and doubt are the springboard to growth. Mature Christians fail forward, as has MacDonald. They say a strategic "no" when others are indulging themselves with "yes," and they fall and learn to get up again. As MacDonald says from his own personal experience, "Mature Christians are experts at repenting and humility." Mature Christians learn under one who has gone before so that "his/her life becomes a textbook on Christ's work in us."

Just like my failed search for a mentor over twenty years ago, young people today are failing to find mentors. People of my genera-

GOD SAVE THE EGGS!

tion are more interested in cruises than model-
ing Christ. As MacDonald puts it, they are "too
busy, too distracted, too secretive, and too
afraid." He doesn't add that they are also too
immature! Maturity in Christ has not been on
the list of baby boomers' long-range goals!

I hope and pray along with Gordon Mac-
Donald that we won't lose a new generation
of young Christians who couldn't get past in-
fancy because we were unwilling or unable to
"emancipate an embryo," or at least share a
recipe!

"Everyone who is human has something to express. Try not expressing yourself for twenty-four hours and see what happens. You will nearly burst. You will want to write a long letter, or draw a picture, or sing…"

Brenda Ueland

Letters from Home

On Thursday Susan went to the post office in our little town of San Isidro de Heredia to pick up the mail. We ("we" meaning Susan) always have to pick up the mail from our box because Costa Rica has no street names and, therefore, no house addresses. This makes home mail delivery a bit challenging.

Challenging, but not impossible.

Some mail actually arrives to us with this address: "1.1 kilometers north of the principal bridge in San Isidro, the black gate three meters high, directly across the street from Cusuco's Bar." This is much better than our former address in Tres Rios. That one was more like: "The old road to Tres Rios, 50 meters east of the electrical sub-station of the ICE (power company), 25 meters north, 25 meters east, 25 meters north. Ask for the tall, bald gringo."

It is hard to come to the place in life where you have become a geographic landmark.

Anyway, Susan went into our little post office where the postmaster (and only employee), Andrea, greeted Susan with an anguished look and the words, "Oh, I am so glad that it is you!" Andrea and Susan usually get along well, so, at the very least, her anguished look caught my wife's attention.

To make a long story short, it seems that over two years ago Andrea took a brief holiday. I vaguely remember the fellow who took her place during the vacation. Unlike Andrea, he wouldn't give me the mail if I showed up without the key for the box. He also apparently put our mail in someone else's box. Now, after two years, that family had finally gotten around to getting the "misdelivered" letters and packages back to Andrea and the Costa Rican postal system. Now we were looking at letters that some of our friends and family had lovingly mailed in 2005!

It is good to know that Arvid and Coleen are not mad at us. They did, in fact, give us their new mailing address when they moved. Of course we wondered why the prayer letters we sent them kept coming back with: "Undeliverable: no forwarding address." That didn't seem like Arv. The 2006 Calendar with beautiful photos and Scripture verses that Dick sent us also finally arrived. It seems a shame to not put it up on a wall someplace. To the rest of you who wrote, I would simply say, "I hope that all of us *did* have a good 2006."

Although, come to think of it, I believe that is when this current U.S. presidential election began in earnest – it couldn't have been *that* good.

This is not the first time we have had interesting mail stories in Latin America.

Once, during a de facto military government in Bolivia, our mail was "held" for three months and read by intelligence agents. I had to visit with a major in the national police force to find out how my mother was doing. He told me she had a summer cold but was getting better.

When we did start getting mail, it wasn't always "all there." One day our daughter Krista received a card from her grandmother with five sticks of gum neatly taped inside. When I picked up the mail and looked in the already-opened envelope, I could see the outside wrapping of those sticks of gum still taped down – without the gum inside! My indignant father blood boiled over. Someone was going to take responsibility for stealing from my daughter this expression of her grandmother's love.

I marched to the office of the director of the post office and demanded that I be allowed to speak directly with him. When he finally came out from his cubby-hole, I think he knew he was in trouble. With righteous anger evident both in my voice and demeanor, I let him know my opinion of people who would steal from a child. I cannot remember if I properly translated the term "lower than a dog that sucks eggs," but I think he caught the gist of my thoughts.

Finally, when I had to take a breath, he said, "Mr. Roland, I know what happened! I can explain it." His apparent willingness to take responsibility stunned me. I waited to hear how he was going to investigate and deal with this evident malfeasance among his employees.

"Mr. Roland, we have had this problem before." He held the envelope up in the air and declared with great conviction, "It is my firm belief that the Mafia in Florida is responsible for stealing this gum."

To this day, the image of two swarthy-looking guys with guns holstered beneath their Armani suits opening greeting cards makes me smile. "Hey, Guido. Look what we have here – chewing gum!"

Without saying another word, I turned on my heel and walked out of his office.

Seriously, we want to thank all of you for your correspondence with us. It is a great encouragement to us. No matter when we receive it.

"From the moment I picked your book up until I laid it down I was convulsed with laughter. Someday I intend reading it."

Julius Henry Marx

What Are You Reading?

I know what you are reading right now! I mean, what are you currently reading in that space you reserve for yourself in your busy life? This question is one I often ask missionaries when I am visiting. I believe a person's "reading diet" provides a window into their soul and well-being.

If nothing else, it makes interesting table conversation.

I am an inveterate reader. I read almost everything – books, newspapers, magazines and catalogs in the pouch in front of me on planes and nearly everything else that has print on it. Just this morning my obsessive-compulsive disorder took over, and I re-read the label on the shampoo I am currently using. "A shampoo guaranteed to luxuriously volumize your hair."

WOODY AND SUSAN ROLAND

First, I doubt that "volumize" is a real word. I bet it wouldn't work in Scrabble. Second, if you have seen a photo of me recently, you can understand why I may doubt the claims this product makes for itself. Apparently there are limits to modern science.

Over breakfast Susan and I enjoy sharing what we have been reading. It is one of the only meals that we regularly get to eat alone. It has become an encouraging time of fellowship for both of us.

This morning I had several of my books at the table in order to share some quotes from my current reading. Susan came armed with a few of her own.

I have been reading *Bonhoeffer Speaks Today* by Mark Devine. It is hard to beat quotes like, "When God calls a man, he bids him come and die." It is hard to deny the stark reality of that statement when you realize Bonhoeffer died eight years after writing those words in Flossenburg... hung by Hitler in a kind of final purge of his enemies.

Henri Nouwen's *The Return of the Prodigal Son* is on my bedside table. Nouwen has been a strange source of quotes for Evangelicals for years.

He wrote, "One of the greatest challenges of the spiritual life is to receive God's forgiveness... Receiving forgiveness requires a total willingness to let God be God and do all the healing, restoring and renewing. As long as I want to do even part of that myself, I end up with partial solutions, such as becoming a hired servant."

Please, Lord, keep me from being a hired servant. Let me be your son.

One of my co-workers, Mark Edwards, is reading with me the book *Living the Life God Has Planned* by Bill Thrasher. I like Thrasher. He is practical, deeply biblical and not too popular. For some reason it always bothers me if the book I am currently reading is too popular. I find it disappointing to find that I might be normal.

Thrasher quotes Tozer when he writes, "What comes to our minds when we think about God is the most important thing about us." If we believed that statement to be true, it would change many of our priorities in study and life.

Susan has been re-reading (once again!) *Rose From Brier* by Amy Carmichael. There are a few great lines in there about books. "I suppose we all have our own familiar book-friends, books that we could not do without. Among mine I name very gratefully *The Pilgrim's Progress*. I do not think that we find the gathered wealth of truth and power and beauty in that book till we read it after life has had time to explain it."

My guess is that we do not understand the power in many books until the truth they contain interacts with our daily lives.

I re-read these thoughts and realize they have gone on far too long for those of you

WOODY AND SUSAN ROLAND

more accustomed to reading email than books. So, let me close with a quote from Brother Lawrence who wrote, "I will pray for you; do you pray instantly for me, who am, in our Lord, yours..."

"Visitor's footfalls are like medicine; they heal the sick."

Bantu Proverb

Visitors

Yesterday we said good-bye to visitors who have been with us for the past week. Chris and Krista returned to Chicago after spending Christmas with us. There is something very special about the anticipation of seeing family during the holiday season. However, as many of you know, the visit is soon over and then you have to say good-bye. I believe the technical explanation of what this feels like is, "It hurts like stink!"

As Krista said to me at the airport yesterday afternoon, "This wouldn't hurt so much if we didn't love each other the way we do."

As the Dufflepuds said in C. S. Lewis' book, *The Voyage of the Dawn Treader*, "That's right! That's right! A truer word has never been spoken."

WOODY AND SUSAN ROLAND

Of course, there are different types of visitors. It hurts when some of them arrive (and stay), and, as I have already mentioned, it really hurts when some visitors leave.

I grew up in a family where you did one of two things on Sundays and holidays. You either received visitors or you "went visiting." Staying home and reading a good book (while not answering your doorbell) was not an option with which I was familiar. This may be why I read so few good books as a child.

We even turned family vacations into extended visits. We would go to northern Minnesota and visit with relatives once or twice removed. As a child I quickly decided that if a relative could not easily be described in terms of cousin, aunt or uncle or long-lost grandparents, then it was better not to ask for detailed explanations. It was easier to limit oneself to, "Yes, I am enjoying school. I learned to swim this year. My sisters treat me well."

If said with an angelic expression, the final statement could result in my sisters actually treating me in said fashion. However, there were never any guarantees.

Once we traveled across the country, accompanied by my great aunt, while visiting other relatives and friends all the way to California. I am not making this up! I think the only place my parents didn't know someone was in Reno, Nevada, and that was probably due to the fact that you could actually gamble there. The only relatives I had who "threw good money after bad" drove something other than John Deere tractors – and there were precious few of them.

Of course we were also the recipients of visits by distant relatives. Many of them were making the pilgrimage back to Minnesota to show their children where they grew up and, possibly, why they left.

I know this is hard for some of you to believe, but even as a child I was outspoken. Sometimes my parents spent as long preparing me for a visit as they did actually cleaning house or baking special desserts. "Woody, please don't bring up your current politics with them. It wouldn't be nice." Being nice in Minnesota was an important cultural value that apparently had a hard time sticking with me.

Once, when my mother was preparing to receive one of those "relatives-not-easily-explained," she invested special time helping me to understand that our visitor was a bit "different." In my mother's lexicon, being different was tantamount to being an alien from outer space. And, to be honest, he *had* gone out East to live, so there might have been some truth to her statement.

I will never forget the day when we were returning from Lake City or Zumbro Falls or some other cultural Mecca of the Midwest. For our relative, it had been a visit within a visit. In our family, this was probably the equivalent of being existentially self-actualized.

I had apparently been at my best behavior.

WOODY AND SUSAN ROLAND

My mother let down her guard and allowed me to sit with our guest in the front seat as she drove. By this time, I was enthralled with him. He knew about books and had even read many of them. He had new ideas. He talked to me in a serious fashion and asked my opinion about current events. Finally, I couldn't hold it in. I turned to my mother and said, "Mom, I don't know what you're talking about. He isn't weird."

It may have been the closest that my mother ever came to driving off the road. My guess is that it turned into one of the few visits in her experience that couldn't end fast enough. I certainly do not remember us making any return visits of our own to this particular relative out East.

I trust that you have some good visits to which you can look forward. I hope you have the privilege of saying with us, "it hurts more to say good-bye than it did to say hello."

"Any successful journey begins by packing your luggage full of imagination."

Katherine Palmer Peterson

Million Mile March

This past week, while traveling from Chicago to Costa Rica with Kari, I reached the one million mile mark with American Airlines. This was noted by my wife when she received an email from the airline congratulating me on the milestone. For some reason, Susan was not as excited or encouraged by this announcement as the airline might have hoped. In fact, she seemed to be somewhat confused as to whether I should be congratulated or she should be consoled.

When I think about one million miles (and I have flown more with other airlines), I am actually surprised by how little has occurred during those hours of sitting with my knees supporting the passenger seat in front of me. Commercial aviation is incredibly safe, and I cannot truthfully remember an "incident" with

WOODY AND SUSAN ROLAND

American in all those miles.

On the other hand, I have had several adventures with two infamous South American airlines. However, both of them are now bankrupt, and I would hate to rub salt in the wound.

I have lost my baggage on three occasions. Each time it has been while traveling through the Miami airport. My guess is that this has more to do with problems in that particular facility than with American Airlines. All of my bags have eventually been found, and other than having to use the same clothes for a few days, I am no worse for the wear or the wearing.

I have been with some interesting people in this million mile march.

I once traveled with an infamous baseball pitcher. He was known for his rather crude comments about some of the cities in which he was "forced" to play. In real life he did not disappoint. At the very least, you could say he was authentic. His private personality was no different than his public persona.

I sat next to a medium-level television star on one trip. Unfortunately, because we have spent so many years in Latin America, I am not always "current" on the latest entertainment personalities. When I did vaguely remember the program on which she had a reoccurring role, the only star on the show I could bring to mind was a dog. I seem to remember her alcohol consumption increased when I began to ask about working with such an interesting canine.

I have met a few famous Christian leaders, authors and personalities on my trips. Apparently their ministries require them to travel a great deal as well. I have helped a well-known preacher through O'Hare airport where his exegetical skills did not seem to be too useful. I have sat next to presidents and directors of ministries. Most of them looked as tired as I felt.

I once chatted for a long time with Joni Erickson Tada while we waited to board a plane in Los Angeles. I did not immediately identify myself as a Christian or as having read any of her books. I was interested in how she would converse with me as a fellow traveler. I must say she did very well – conversation filled with grace. Later, when I identified myself as a missionary, she said, "I knew there was something different about you!"

Many of you would agree with the statement if not her exact meaning.

I always pray for the passenger who will be seated next to me on the flight. I ask God to permit me to have the right conversation at the right time. It is my intention to be salt even if no meals are being served on that segment.

Once, while returning from a rather long and difficult trip in Latin America, I was upgraded to business class. I was looking forward to having food that did not come out of a foil packet. Unfortunately, there are certain predictable effects that travel in some South American countries have on the human digestive system. While still waiting for the plane to begin taxiing to the runway, I began to feel some of those familiar pains in my nether regions.

It was at this moment that the affluent business man seated next to me asked me what I do for a living. Through gritted teeth I said, "I am a missionary." He opened his eyes wide and presented an incredible opening. "I am successful in business and miserable in life. Can you tell me how to find peace with God?"

I had just finished the part of God loving us and having real interest in having fellowship with each one of us when we reached straight and level and the seat belt sign went off. My traveling companion asked me, "Woody, if this is true why don't I have this kind of meaningful relationship with God?" I am afraid I had to encourage him to hold that question while I leapt towards the bathroom.

For the rest of the flight, we alternated between questions, answers and explosive trips to the bathroom. I couldn't eat any of the food that was served. The other passengers in business class expressed their disgust at my monopoly of the bathroom with their pointed looks each time I returned to my seat. My new friend only seemed interested in understanding the Gospel.

I sometimes wonder what became of him

and if he ever shares his testimony of the leaping missionary. I hope so. If I were him, I certainly would.

Robert Frost wrote:

"The woods are lovely, dark, and deep,
But I have promises to keep,
And miles to go before I sleep,
And miles to go before I sleep."

I understand those words. God has given me the privilege of traveling many miles. There are many more ahead. I only pray that He permits me to arrive home before it gets dark.

"Man has to suffer. When he has no real afflictions, he invents some."

Jose Martí

It Doesn't Hurt That Bad

Sometimes people have strange ideas about missions. It seems like there is a type of regressive DNA within Evangelical Christianity that causes people to think that all missionaries are suffering incredible problems because of their involvement in the *Every Day Commission*. Missions are the final resting place for masochists within modern Christianity.

I hate to break it to you, but it is just not that way. Well, most of the time. The truth is, it doesn't hurt that bad.

Now, in the interest of full-disclosure during this political season, I should say that Susan and I have been through a few moments during our thirty years in missions.

We have both had hepatitis. I can assure you that sharing the hospital room together

211

was not the high point of our marital communication. We have both had paratyphoid fever. Again and again and again. For the purpose of this public document, we will not mention how many times we have had salmonelosis and the natural results that bacteria has on the human body. I will only say it wasn't pretty and it wasn't fun.

Of course, there were the revolutions and the times people tried make a political point by shooting at us. It wasn't personal. It was more like a case of "wrong time, wrong place." In retrospect, that was probably as true for the shooters as it was for us, the "shootees."

I am reminded of the prayers required for those serving with the British Army during WWII. Official grace at mealtime was: "O Lord, for what we are about to receive, may we be truly thankful." I believe I prayed something similar at the beginning of each revolution we went through.

Although we have also had the random sting or snake bite, the thing that has hurt the most during these years has been separation from others. Disease, revolution and venomous creatures are not comfortable, but they are not nearly as bad as being a long way off from all of you.

We miss our daughters more than I can express in these poor lines. We enjoyed the girls when they were at home, and we have missed them every single day since they started their own lives and ministries.

We miss our families. Uncles and aunts die; cousins go on with their own lives; nieces and nephews grow up hearing about that daft uncle they have in Latin America but can't remember meeting. Now that kind of thing hurts.

There has been the odd persecution for our faith. Traditional cultures with traditional religions often respond with a bit of tension to new ideas. It doesn't matter how good those new ideas might be.

I have had a few people yell at me because of being a Christian. I remember one old man who used every swear word he could think of for me. Finally, as he tried to catch his breath in the mountain air, he screamed, "You, you are an... (gasp) Evangelical!" If that was the worst thing he could think of, I guess I am going to survive.

Once, while walking in Afghanistan, a group of children and young teenagers identified me as a foreigner and threw rocks at me. It was a good thing that I could still run in those days. Some of them had good arms and big rocks. Still, I like to think they probably persecuted me because I looked different and not because they disagreed with my theology.

I think most of you reading this think that Christians have the right to be treated with respect along with all the other major religions. However, the Bible tells us something different.

We will be insulted. If we stand up for righteousness, we will be called intolerant. If we stand up for brotherhood, we will be called fools.

We will be persecuted. It may be blatant, as it is in many parts of the world where just being a Christian is illegal. It may be subtle, as it is in many corporations where being a Christian is a bar to promotion. But it will be there.

We will be falsely accused. The wildest of tales will circulate. Urban legends will be told as fact and taken as truth because "experts" say so.

What are we supposed to do with all of this? Rejoice.

James tells us that we are actually to count it "pure joy" when we go through this. Why? Maybe because the reality in your life has resulted in Satan seeing you as a worthy opponent – and God has confirmed it. After all, he wouldn't allow you to go through it if you were not able to withstand it. It is a badge of honor. Maybe the only one we will ever get in this world as Christians.

Now, there are a few limitations in all this. First, the suffering must be for His sake. If I am suffering because of my own stupidity, it may be that I am simply being disciplined by the one who loves me. Second, the accusations must be false. If we find ourselves being punished for crimes we have actually done, there is no joy or honor in that.

When we do go through hard times, we should remember that we are in good company.

GOD SAVE THE EGGS!

All the original disciples I know about (except John) died rather grisly, R-rated deaths. The same thing could be said of most of the prophets. Their words came from God, and their suffering was their service to that same God. It was not the words that made them great. It was their faithful suffering as they communicated those words.

When I was a teenager, I wanted to make the varsity football team more than anything. The irony was the day I was told that I had finally made the starting lineup, I quit. I had just discovered the joy of aviation, and I wasn't going to let anything stand in my way of becoming a pilot.

When I think of those prophets suffering, when I think of the early disciples, when I go through occasional hard times because of my own faith, I realize that I have finally made the varsity team. I have finally made the first-string.

This time I need to continue on in the game.